At David C Cook, we equip the local church around the corner and around the globe to make disciples. Come see how we are working together—go to **www.davidccook.com**. Thank you!

transforming lives together

What people are saying about …

Walk It Out

"Tricia Goyer lives a life that will challenge readers to step up and walk out faith in our homes, communities, and the world, and ultimately experience all the joy promised when we are in His will and doing His work."

—**Francine Rivers**, *New York Times* bestselling author
of more than thirty novels, including *Redeeming Love*

"For several decades, I have watched Tricia and her family take large and small steps of faith. If God said it, they did it. Every time the results have been extraordinary. I'm so glad she's captured the best of those experiences in this practical, deeply inspirational book. She demonstrates how, when we listen and do what God asks us to do, He always provides, directs, and blesses us many times over. If you need motivation to get your life back on the path that leads to joy and great hope, grab this book and 'walk it out.' A radically changed life awaits you!"

—**Robin Jones Gunn**, bestselling author
of *Victim of Grace* and *Spoken For*

"Tricia Goyer doesn't just walk it out; she compels us to do the same. This is one of those rare books that changes you. There is no abstract spirituality within these pages. *Walk It Out* is practical and inspiring for every reader who needs to know what it means to follow Jesus in the everyday moments of life."

—**Amber Lia**, bestselling author of *Triggers: Exchanging Parents' Angry Reactions for Gentle Biblical Responses*

"I didn't get past the introduction of *Walk It Out* before my heart was moved and soul shaken by the words of an everyday woman who decided to just want God. I hope hundreds of thousands of people read this book. It's that important. Tricia Goyer truly walks out every word of this true story turned guidebook of the surrendered Jesus life. May deep call to deep and move us all to such obedience. Gratefully, I endorse this powerful book."

—**Lisa Whittle**, speaker, author of *I Want God* and *Put Your Warrior Boots On*

"*Walk It Out* is compelling, thought-provoking, and encouraging. Tricia takes readers through her personal journey to discover what it meant for her family to truly walk out Scriptures that instruct us all to care for the 'least of these,' while inviting all of us to move away from our comfort zones and into God's will. A must-read for anyone who needs a reminder that serving is not about a bigger to-do list or striving but about a deeper connection with Jesus."

—**Crystal Stine**, freelance writer, communications consultant, author of *Creative Basics* and *Holy Hustle* (fall 2018)

"Tricia Goyer doesn't dictate how you 'should' live by faith in God's Word. She walks it out. Sharing her own redeemed struggles, Tricia guides your heart to embrace Jesus's unique purposes and helps you 'take hold of the life that is truly life.'"

—**Heather MacFadyen**, creator and host of the GodCenteredMom podcast

"Many of us have the desire to follow God, but few of us actually know how to. I can't think of a better person to show us through her inspiring life story than Tricia Goyer. *Walk It Out* will give you a first-hand look at what a life, even through the most trying circumstances, genuinely lived for God actually looks like!"

—**Ruth Schwenk**, founder of TheBetterMom.com,
cofounder of FortheFamily.org, coauthor of
Pressing Pause and *For Better or For Kids*

"Hindsight is always 20/20, but *Walk It Out* is a gift of foresight—one of those rare finds that prepares you for what is to come, and helps you right where you are today. While providing a look ahead, Tricia's new book helps you learn to recognize your defining moments or turning points as they happen, and she shows you how to respond in faith instead of fear."

—**Amanda Bennett**, author and speaker

"If anyone has walked out their faith by leaning on the Word of God, it's Tricia. Fully knowing the only book we need in life is the Bible, it sure is helpful having a trusted friend like Tricia to demonstrate how she's done this in her own life and guide us to do the same in our own."

—**Sami Cone**, blogger and media personality,
bestselling author of *Raising Uncommon Kids*

"Tricia has written a beautiful guidebook that takes our hands and shows us how we can follow God beyond our comfort zones—where life really begins. Filled with powerful stories from her own life and practical wisdom she learned along the way, Tricia inspires and equips us to live out our faith no matter our season or situation."

—**Kat Lee**, author of *Maximize Your Mornings*,
founder and director of HelloMornings.org

"*Walk It Out* is my favorite kind of book: one that makes you reach for your highlighter and dog ear its pages. Tricia Goyer shares her story with an honesty that inspires me to be more vulnerable in my own life; she shows us that revealing our brokenness can lead to healing and forgiveness and can help us to help others. The priorities she outlines for her family are so good I sat down and discussed them with my husband. Tricia presents real ways, both large and small, to translate belief into action. If you yearn to live out your faith and discover how God can use you to make a difference here on earth. I highly recommend this book."

—**Dawn Camp**, editor and photographer of *The Beauty of Grace, The Gift of Friendship*, and *The Heart of Marriage*

"From the moment I first met Tricia, her life has challenged me to look at my own life differently. What is God's Word clearly calling me to do? How can I live out His desires for me daily? Where is fear holding me back from stepping out more boldly for Him? *Walk It Out* beautifully illustrates what can happen in our lives when we surrender our plans and dreams and embrace the path God has for us—regardless of how many bumps there have been on the road behind us. Within the pages of this life-changing book, we hear about Tricia's story and even catch glimpses of where some of the heroines in her fictional books may have gotten their inspiration. We get to experience how God used the good, the bad, and the ugly parts of her life to bring about His glory and His love to so many lives. It's simply amazing!"

—**Kristi Clover**, author of *Sanity Savers for Moms* and coauthor of *Homeschool Basics*, speaker, blogger, host of the Simply Joyful podcast

"Is the gospel merely a set of abstract doctrines to be believed? Or is it a message that transforms the heart and finds its expression in the way we live every day? Tricia Goyer contends for a Christianity with hands and feet that reaches out to the lost and the hurting. Both convicting and compassionate, this book will challenge you to not merely hear the Word, but to do what it says."

—**Israel Wayne**, author, conference speaker, director of Family Renewal

"If you prefer remain distanced from God's tangible presence and power in your life, then you might want to grab a different book. If you ache to experience God's nearness and activity in a way that takes your breath away, however, then *Walk It Out* by Tricia Goyer just might be your best next step. Lean in, friend, and discover the kind of life only God could orchestrate."

—**Michele Cushatt**, author of *I Am: A 60-Day Journey to Knowing Who You Are Because of Who He Is*

"There is no person I'd rather hear from on the topic of walking out my faith than Tricia Goyer. Her life speaks volumes about obedience to God's call, trusting Him in the process, and as a result, doing radically uncomfortable things. So it follows that she offers a trusted and honest guide in navigating *how* to walk out your faith in her newest book *Walk It Out*. This is not a book on living a perfect life. It's a book for those of us stumbling through our days wondering if we can do anything meaningful for God during our short lives. A book for those of us afraid of what God might say or where He might send us when we say, 'Lord send me.' I offer my wholehearted endorsement for *Walk It Out*."

—**Alexandra Kuykendall**, author of *Loving My Actual Life* and cohost The Open Door Sisterhood podcast

TRICIA GOYER

walk it out

THE RADICAL RESULT OF LIVING GOD'S WORD ONE STEP AT A TIME

David C Cook

transforming lives together

WALK IT OUT
Published by David C Cook
4050 Lee Vance Drive
Colorado Springs, CO 80918 U.S.A.

David C Cook U.K., Kingsway Communications
Eastbourne, East Sussex BN23 6NT, England

The graphic circle C logo is a registered trademark of David C Cook.

LCCN 2017933741
ISBN 978-1-4347-1099-4
eISBN 978-1-4347-1110-6

Published in association with the Books & Such Literary Management, 52 Mission
Circle, Suite 122, PMB 170, Santa Rosa, CA 95409-5370, www.booksandsuch.com.

The Team: Alice Crider, Liz Heaney, Amy Konyndyk, Nick Lee, Diane
Gardner, Rachael Stevenson, Carol Ann Hiemstra, Susan Murdock
Cover Design: Tim Green, Faceout Studio
Cover Photo: Getty Images

Printed in the United States of America

First Edition 2017
1 2 3 4 5 6 7 8 9 10

072617

To John—I'm so thankful God has brought you into my life to walk this journey together. You always inspire me to walk out what I feel God is putting on my heart through His Word. Thank you for your love and your support. I can't imagine a more perfect partner to travel through life with.

Contents

Foreword

I'll never forget the day I met Tricia Goyer. The owner of our local Christian bookstore told me, "You need to meet Tricia. She's a writer too."

I had no idea this woman would become so influential in my life. To be hones, when we first met, I was intimidated. Ten years younger than me, Tricia seemed to have it all together.

She already had an agent shopping her first novel. In between writing regularly for Christian magazines, she homeschooled her three kids and created children's church curriculum that she and her husband taught each week. On top of that, her house was immaculate!

Me on the other hand? Well, I was a pastor's wife who felt called to write but never seemed to get around to it, a mother who loved her children deeply but prayed passionately she'd never have to homeschool, and a recovering slob who couldn't remember the last time her home was even close to immaculate.

Tricia's gentle kindness, however, melted away my feelings of inadequacy. As we talked, it became clear this woman was passionate about writing. She'd found her purpose and was working hard to fulfill her dream. But not in a driven, look-at-me sort of way. That's not Tricia at all. (I've never met a humbler person.) Instead, as we grew closer, I watched Tricia consistently do the hard work of writing, calmly persevering and trusting God even when publishing doors slammed shut.

Eventually, those doors opened (boy, did they open!), but over the years I've watched Tricia regularly set aside her dreams so she could follow Jesus. Saying yes to God over and over, even when it meant turning her perfectly ordered life upside down. Stretching an already full and busy life to make room for another piece of God's will. It's been breathtaking and beautiful to behold.

At first, Tricia was my writing mentor. But over the years, she's mentored my *life* as well. Showing me what it looks like to lay down my life rather than save it. How to love and serve people, not just in word but in tangible, life-giving ways. How to step out in faith when God calls, fully believing He'll lead and empower me as I go.

In this book you'll be inspired to do the same—to be more available to God than ever before—but expect to be challenged as well. *Walk It Out* has certainly challenged me as I've read its pages. There are points I'm still mulling over with Jesus.

Please don't rush through this book. Let the stories and Scriptures probe any unsurrendered corners in your heart. Make notes in the margin. Take time to journal through the questions at the end of each chapter. Be honest with yourself and with God. Dialogue with Jesus, inviting Him into any resistance you may feel. Ask Him to make you willing to follow no matter where He leads. Invite the

Holy Spirit to give you wisdom as to what steps of obedience He wants you to take.

In this process of putting feet to your faith, you are never alone. Philippians 2:13 reminds us, "For it is God who works in you to will and to act in order to fulfill his good purpose."

Isn't that great news, my friend? God *works it in*. And because of His enabling power, you and I can *walk it out*.

Happy trails!

> —Joanna Weaver, bestselling author of *Having a Mary Heart in a Martha World: Finding Intimacy with God in the Busyness of Life*

Acknowledgments

This book started on a drive from my home in Little Rock, Arkansas, to Dallas, Texas, where I was attending a conference. My editor, life coach, and friend, Alice Crider, had just been hired for a role at David C Cook, and I was calling to congratulate her. As we talked, I updated her on everything God was doing in my life. I told her about the inner-city church we were attending, the teen moms I was mentoring, and the children we were adopting. I shared how God had impressed it on my heart to come to His Word with the conviction that I was to just do what it said, no matter the cost.

"This sounds like a book," Alice's encouraging voice said on the other end of the line. "I know the title—*Walk It Out.*" A chill raced up my arms as she said those words, and I knew she was spot on. A few days later I spoke with my agent, Janet Grant, who agreed with Alice. I stood there, amazed to receive the confirmation that the journey John and I were on wasn't just for me but for readers too.

If it wasn't for Alice, Janet, my editor Liz, and the amazing team at David C Cook, you wouldn't be holding this book in your hands.

And if it wasn't for my husband, John, our children, our friends, and our community, I wouldn't have anything to write about. This book happened because I had an editor and agent who urged me to share the steps God was leading John and me on. But this journey also happened because God surrounded John and me with friends and family who pray for us and care for us as we step out to do all we feel God is calling us to do.

My heart is full of thankfulness for our neighbors, Tracey Loyd, Bruce and Cindy Mauer, and Chris and Laura Walker, who truly walk out this journey with us as they've helped with our kids on numerous occasions. I'm thankful for my assistant, Christen Krumm, who makes me look as if I can do it all, even when she's doing most of it. I'm thankful for my number one prayer supporters: Tracy Steel, Kristi Clover, Rebecca Ondov, Teri Lynne Underwood, Rebecca Altman, Amber Lia, and Cindy Coloma, who I know I can text day or night and they will pray. I'm thankful for the staff and friends of Mosaic Church in Little Rock, especially Harry Li, Mike Clowers, Deb Salder, Cai Lane, Alex and Erin Diaz, and Stephen and Alicia Geppert, who involve themselves in our lives to provide all types of support that our family needs. And I'm thankful for Mary Lester, who volunteered to tutor Maria and turned into a dear friend.

I wouldn't be doing Teen MOPS without Jan Jeffery, Lottie Jernigan, Jennifer Gonzales, Shamim Okollah, Georgia Morris, Benilda Tillman, and Brooke Montgomery. You're all amazing leaders and mentors. And John and I are thankful for our best friends Kenny and Twyla Klundt, who actually think it's fun to go on vacations with our big, crazy family!

I'm thankful for the caring therapists at All Children's Academy and the Child Study Center, both of Little Rock, Arkansas. You've guided me and helped in providing tools for healing for my kids. I'm also thankful for my Coeur d'Alene writer friends and my Mastermind Group who continually encourage all my writing and lift me up in prayer. And I'm filled with love and deep gratitude for our church family in Vysoke Myto and Olomouc, Czech Republic, who love and care for our daughter Leslie so well.

Finally, I have to acknowledge my older kids Cory and Kate, Leslie and Honza, and Nathan for urging Dad and me to open our home to these kids. You truly are our biggest helpers and prayer warriors. And for all our other kids—Maria, Lauren, Jordan, Florentina, Bella, Alyssa, and Casey—what a great God to bring you into our lives! And our bonus daughters and son-in-law—Kayleigh, Andrea, Lili, and Regi—our lives wouldn't be complete without you. Finally, my grandkids—MaCayla, Audrie, Donovan, Clayton, Chloe, Maya, Te'o, and Adrianna—I can't wait to see what God will do in your lives and in future generations as we continue to walk out His Word for His glory!

Living the Life I Never Dreamed

I wish you could see me right now, sitting on my bed with my laptop. If you showed up at my house, my bedroom would be the last place I'd want you to see … for good reason. It's a mess. I'm not talking about a clothes-on-the-floor or a-dirty-cup-on-the-nightstand mess. I mean a plastic-bins-filled-with-books-blockading-the-side-of-the-bed mess, which means I have to crawl from the foot of the bed to my pillow to get into bed. Three two-foot-high piles of dust-covered research books perch atop my dresser. We crammed a desk into this room too; it's littered with kids' homework papers, therapy schedules, writing projects, and psychiatrist's notes. I dig around for ten minutes just to find anything, and sometimes I don't discover it on the desk, but in one of the piles on the floor.

Where did this mess come from? I've authored more than sixty books, and since I started writing twenty years ago, I've worked at home. A year and a half ago John and I cleared out my home office and library and hauled it all into our bedroom. We did this because our four new daughters needed rooms. (We were adopting them from foster care at the ages of ten, twelve, twelve, and fifteen.) So out went my desk, chair, books, bookshelves, and files, all to be stuffed into our small bedroom. And in went bunk beds, dressers, and all things teen girl.

The girls moved in the first week of summer 2015, arriving with a truckload of stuff. They had lots of clothes. Some fit them, most didn't. They also brought lots of toys and mementos—gifts from former foster parents, generous churches, and thoughtful sponsors who had drawn the girls' names from holiday trees. They still had a few things from their biological mom's house, from which they had been removed six years prior. The girls came with a lot of internal baggage too, but I'll dig into all that later in this book.

This is my life. It's not the life this type A, neat freak, firstborn ever thought she'd be living. Yet it's one I wouldn't trade for the world. Because to give up the chaos would be to give up these kids. It would be to give up the books I'm writing and the ministries that bring joy to my heart. It would be to give up the purpose I've discovered as I've followed Jesus one step at a time.

To be clear, the chaos is more seen than felt. The rest of the family doesn't seem to mind stepping over eleven pairs of kicked-off shoes every time they enter the front door. This place I call a mess, my kids now call home. Clutter and all, our adopted children have found a place where they're completely loved and accepted. And that, I've discovered, is worth climbing over the end of my bed before collapsing onto my pillow every night, at least for now.

HOW I GOT HERE

I was at the lowest of low points when I became a Christian in 1989, but when I turned my life over to Jesus, a glimmer of hope inside told me He had something good planned for me. Actually, He had more planned than I could even imagine then.

In addition to the four adopted daughters I mentioned, John and I have six other kids (three biological and three others also adopted). When I'm not washing mountains of laundry or cooking army-sized portions of dinner, I travel, speak (sometimes in other countries), and write—books, blog posts, and articles for national publications. I've helped start a crisis pregnancy center and lead a teen mom support group in inner-city Little Rock. I neither planned nor expected any of this—from the ten kids to the stamped-up passport. I didn't accomplish these things by making a list and checking it off. They happened as I heard God's voice and took steps of faith to follow His directives. Radical, right?

I've dedicated myself to following God, reading His Word, and doing what it says. Following Him has led me to do things I never expected, and along the way I've experienced a deep sense of purpose. What is that purpose? It isn't just one thing. Instead it is a fluid mixture of callings that God reveals as I see Him at work in this world and dare to step into the good work He's designed for me. It wasn't that I needed to do good things to *earn* love or salvation, but instead I do them because I'm committed to giving all of myself to God. I trust in God's love and saving grace. I trust and follow Him as He leads me in His perfect will. I've learned that God's good plans are not always easy or neat, but when we step out in obedience we never walk alone.

I remember sitting down to my personal quiet time with a pile of books one morning. I'd been studying and learning a lot, but I felt I was barely scratching the surface, and I was frustrated.

Then, as I opened one of my study books, I sensed God's Spirit whisper, "Are you done learning about Me, and are you ready to connect with Me?" At first it surprised me. After all, isn't Bible study a good thing? Then I realized I was filling my mind with head knowledge, and God now wanted me to place my feet on the ground and walk out my faith, to *act*. He wanted me to have a living faith that was undeniable to me and to all those He brought into my life.

"It's today I must be livin'," wrote Catherine Marshall, one of my favorite authors.[1] For so long I'd built up that Bible knowledge to prepare for whatever future ministry God had in store, but God's Spirit said, "*The time to act is now*. There is a world in need of Me. It's not about knowing the Word; it's about living it *today*."

As believers we often have our morning devotions, go to Bible study with friends, faithfully attend church and listen to sermons, read Christian books, and stream Christian music and podcasts. Yet we are missing Jesus. We forget to pay attention to the things that are breaking God's heart, and instead we order our world as much as possible for ease, comfort, and success. Instead of posting our favorite inspirational passages on Facebook, Instagram, or Pinterest, we need to search the Scriptures with more diligence and attention. And then we need to do what it says.

When I began to walk out Scripture's mandates—to care for the orphan and the widow, serve the poor, take the good news into all the world, and so on—God sparked passions within me I never knew existed. My life became the radical result of living God's Word one step at a time. It didn't happen overnight, but looking back I see God's hand guiding me, bringing me to this full house and abundant, overflowing life.

When Scripture's mandates directed my life, I discovered a God-designed mission that has excited and delighted me. God worked miracles in and through me, some I'll share within the pages of this book. He has more in store for me, more passions to spark, more mandates to fulfill, more miracles to perform. I'm still walking this journey, and I welcome you to join me.

Of course, the directives within these pages aren't exhaustive. These are simply the areas God has addressed in my life. These are the Scriptures He's used to direct my path, one truth at a time. As I share what God has done in and through me as I've walked out His Word, I hope to help you discover how He can do something similar in and through *you*. God has a purpose for you, one greater than you ever imagined. The road won't always be easy, though you may experience seasons of happy chaos along the way, but His purpose for your life is one that will not only fulfill you but will also benefit the world.

Are you exhausted from doing "good things" for God yet still feel unfulfilled? Does it seem as if you've lost your sense of purpose? Do you believe God has big plans for your life, but you just can't seem to get there? Do you wonder about the "great purpose" God has designed for you?

If you identify with any of these questions, you're in the right place. I've asked all these questions myself. And while I don't have perfect answers, I've discovered many truths along the way. I'm excited to take this journey with you. I pray you'll discover more about your own purpose along the way, step-by-step, with Jesus by your side.

1

That Defining Moment

Growing up I knew exactly what I wanted in life. I wanted to get married and live in the small Northern California town I was being raised in. I wanted kids. I wanted to be a teacher so I could be home in the afternoon, enjoy regular family dinners around the table, and spend summers splashing in snow-fed Lake Siskiyou.

Back then, I'd float on my back on hot summer days, kicking softly as I gazed at the wide, blue sky, and dream about my future husband, future kids, and future students. I believed my life's purpose was to be a dedicated wife and mom, to raise well-behaved children, and to be an inspiring teacher. I had a dream and purpose in mind, but things didn't turn out like I'd expected.

When I was seventeen and a high school senior, I discovered I was pregnant—again. The first time I'd had an abortion, and I felt enormous guilt, regret, and shame as a result.[1] I knew abortion wasn't the answer and decided to keep my baby this time. I dropped out of school because I couldn't hide what I'd done, and because I didn't want to see my baby's father with his new girlfriend. I walked away from cheerleading and my friends. I sank into depression and slept most days. I didn't want to think about the future. I didn't want to picture my life as a single mom. Deep down I had no hope.

I had pretty much given up on myself. But there were a few women who loved me and refused to give up on me. These women, who were in my mother's and grandmother's Bible study, prayed for me and invited me to study the Bible with them. They even gave me a baby shower. I felt unworthy of their love and smiles, but their love and warmth were a soothing balm to my soul.

One day, when I was six months along, I woke up in my usual miserable state, but I didn't stay that way. Instead of thinking about how I'd messed up my life, I started thinking about those women and their love for me. *If they love me despite what I've done, maybe God does too*, I thought. I dared to hope that He did.

I grew up in church, and I believed in God, but in my teen years I did my own thing. I didn't want to think too hard about Him or how I was living. I had a huge hole in my heart, and I sought love in all the wrong places. But the boys I gave myself to hurt me again and again, and soon I built a wall of bricks around my heart, guarding my bruised and tender emotions from further hurt. The love of those women opened a small crack in that wall, one just wide enough for a single shaft of light to flood my heart. The love of ordinary women opened me up to the love of a not-so-ordinary God.

That morning I wrapped my arms around my pregnant body and prayed, *God, I screwed up this time. If You can do anything with my life, please do.* (Yes, it was a very eloquent prayer.) At that moment God's light filled my heart, and love poured in. I was different—alive and hopeful—and I dedicated myself to living for God. I'd tried traveling down my own path—seeking to gratify my body and heart—and it had brought me pain and heartache. Now, I was ready to discover God's purpose for me. I wanted to do things His way. My new dream was to live as God wanted me to: as a good and faithful daughter.

From that moment of humility, desperation, and need, I trusted God with my future. His hopes and dreams for me were surely better than the life I'd been living! I started praying for a husband, and two weeks after my son Cory was born, God brought me John, an amazing man who loved me, and loved my son, but mostly loved the Lord. We married and a few years later, John and I had two more kids. I was thankful for the new life God had given me, and that the hurting, downcast woman I used to be was a thing of the past.

God had transformed my life, and I focused on doing all I could to serve Him. I was determined to be the perfect wife and mom and that we would be the perfect Christian family. We attended church services on Sundays and midweek. We joined a small group and surrounded ourselves with Christian friends. I volunteered as a children's Sunday school teacher and attended Bible studies. If such a thing as a Christian Service Award existed, I would have been at the top of the list of nominees.

But in time I became aware of an emptiness inside me. If my purpose was to be a good and faithful child of God, why did I feel a spiritual void? I was doing all the right things, but I still felt woefully unfulfilled. I was working so hard to be good, but I never felt good enough.

God, isn't there more to the Christian life than this? I prayed.

MISSING THE MARK

Maybe you're like me. Maybe you thank God for all He has rescued you from (mainly yourself and your destructive choices), and you want to do everything you can to serve Him. But maybe, also like me, it just doesn't seem to be enough.

"I know I'm doing what God has called me to do, but I feel like I'm missing the intimacy of my relationship with Him," my friend Kimberly confessed. "I feel like I'm so busy doing what is right, that I'm missing a deeper connection."

Another friend, Martha, understands Kimberly's frustration. "I remember asking God how I was supposed to keep up with all the good things I was doing for Him for the many years to come. That was the point I realized He didn't need me to do the things I considered to be good. If I allow my 'well doing' to consume me and forget why I do it or for whom I am working, I am working in vain. God needs my heart more than my deeds."

And then there are those who've done it all and are disoriented and discontent with their new season of life. My friend Emma Mae feels this way. She used to volunteer with me at church and for vacation Bible school. She could be counted on—often the first to be called on to volunteer—but now her health keeps her from doing all she used to do. On top of that, her kids are grown and she is a widow. Emma Mae told me, "I feel useless. Not needed anymore."

Can you relate? Do you think:

- *I'm doing all I know to do for God, but I feel as if I'm missing Him.*

- *I can't keep up this pace. Everything feels empty, meaningless.*
- *I can't do all I used to do. I feel useless, not needed anymore.*

I suspect many of us feel unfulfilled in our Christian walk. We are simply surviving, sensing we are missing out on God's big plan. We have an inkling that He has more for us, but we don't know how to get from where we are to "there." We wonder if we'll ever realize our potential, hoping God has more for us than this.

Because we feel empty and see our efforts as meaningless, we work harder to fill the hole deep inside us. We believe if we do certain things and live a certain way, we'll feel happy and fulfilled as a follower of God. So we join another Bible study or volunteer for one more ministry, hoping it will provide the answer our souls have been longing for. We strive, believing that if we do all the right things we'll eventually get what we want: peace, fulfillment, and a close relationship with God. We take notes during the pastor's sermon, but then wake up Monday morning to the same routine. We read Christian living books and pore over Sunday school lessons to increase our knowledge about God, but that knowledge doesn't translate into actionable steps in our everyday lives.

We do all we know to do, but our hearts still cry out: *You're missing the mark.*

It's the last thing we want to hear, especially if we've been striving and serving. After all, if Christian service doesn't fulfill us, what will?

Here's the thing: working *for* God never gives us the depth of connection we desire, no matter how noble our efforts. Consequently, we either question God or believe we're doing something wrong (while everyone else is getting it right, of course). So we try even harder. But that never makes things better. If anything it just makes us more tired.

In our day and age, many Western Christians have Bible knowledge, but don't understand how to translate that knowledge into a true connection with Jesus. We go to Bible study and do the homework, yet we feel jealous and a bit cynical when we see God using other people and not us. Many of us are wandering through life, wondering if what we're doing matters.

TIME TO WALK IT OUT

Everything changed in my life when I stopped focusing on my own dreams and purposes, and instead concentrated on walking out God's dreams and purposes for my life. That may sound like an elusive goal. You may wonder how you can even know God's purposes for you in the first place, but they are easier to discover than you might think.

It comes down to this: Rather than trying to determine what study we should join, book we should read, or ministry we should get involved with, we should instead ask God to break our hearts with the things that break His. Rather than just reading God's Word for personal and group study, we should actually *do* what it says—even the really hard things. This is where we find our joy, our purpose. Not by coming up with our own ideas about how we are to live as God's daughters, but by taking faith steps daily, believing that as we seek God's face He'll invite us to join Him in His work. Not by trying to decipher the future He has for us, but instead by trusting that even though the path doesn't make sense now, we'll look back over the years and realize He's been directing us all along.

These are all lessons I've learned over the last twenty-eight years as a Christian. I've allowed God to break my heart and change my dreams and purposes so they align with the clear directives in His Word. I've learned to have faith that God's Word will not lead me astray. I've learned to be okay with not knowing the big picture and to trust Him with every step of faith.

What God has accomplished through me always amazes people, and they want to know how I do it all. First, I don't do it all. I've just committed to reading God's Word and walking it out. Second, when I take these steps to walk out God's Word, He provides me with all I need to fulfill His call. Whether you realize it or not, God intended for us to do what the Bible says: take the gospel into all the world, care for the vulnerable, help the needy, tend to our most important relationships. These are guideposts that point us down the path of true living and eternal life.

"I used to ask God to help me," said Hudson Taylor, humble missionary and founder of the China Inland Mission. "Then I asked if I might help Him. I ended up by asking Him to do His work through me."[2] These words resonate with me, because God took me on the same journey from independence to dependence.

THE TURNING POINT

In everyone's story, there comes a defining moment when life takes a turn. I didn't see the twist coming, and looking back it almost seems too ordinary an event to be considered "the moment." But as I ponder all that has happened since then, I have no doubt that everything changed one quiet, early morning in 1999—the morning I said yes to what I knew God was asking me to do.

Earlier that year I had faced one of the hardest losses of my life. My eighty-three-year-old grandfather had lost his battle with cancer. I had been his caregiver after he and my grandmother moved into our home. I'd see the gates of death, but I'd also witnessed what the Bible means in Psalm 116:15: "Precious in the sight of the LORD is the death of his faithful servants." I'll share more about this later.

After his death my life had returned to normal, or so I thought. I was twenty-eight years old, married, a mother of three, and had just signed a book contract. In the few years before this point, I had attended a Bible study for women who'd had abortions and faced the pain and shame of my past. Now once a week I was teaching a post-abortion Bible study and seeing women from all walks of life find freedom in Christ. Freedom from regret. Freedom from self-loathing. Freedom from hiding and the feeling that God could never forgive them or use them.

In this window of my life, when I'd just tasted heaven and was walking with a new confidence as a beloved daughter of God, my pastor approached me.

"Tricia, I feel God asking me to help start a crisis pregnancy center in our town, and knowing your heart and story I want to know if you can help," he said.

Gulp.

I told Pastor Daniel I'd pray about it, knowing full well that answer was a delay tactic. I had no intention of doing any such thing. My life was full. I was homeschooling our kids, writing every morning before the rest of the family woke up, and leading a Bible study. My life had reached a wonderful balance of service to my church, to my community, and to my family. I couldn't envision taking on one more thing.

Yet the next morning as I pulled out my Bible to do my devotions, something stirred in my heart. Looking back, I realize the Holy Spirit was reminding me that I actually needed to *pray* about Pastor Daniel's request. I'm a little embarrassed now but my prayer went something like this: *Dear God, I thank You for what You've done with my life. I told Pastor Daniel that I'd pray about this crisis pregnancy center, but please show me how to tell him that I don't have time for that. I'm homeschooling my kids and teaching them about You. I'm writing articles and now a book, and my words are going around the world, teaching others about You. So this is something I just can't do …*

Immediately a thought entered my mind that I knew wasn't my own: *What about the young women who feel just like you did—scared and uncertain of where to turn? Don't you remember the women who reached out to share love with you during your darkest time? Where would you be without them? And what are you going to do about the young women who need love and truth right within your own community? How are you going to help them as you were helped?*

Double gulp.

I knew what God was asking me to do. He had a dream and a purpose for me. Both were greater than anything I had ever imagined. And that dream and purpose wasn't just about what He wanted for *me* but also about what He wanted for the *women in my community*.

Immediately two verses came to mind, ones I'd memorized as a child: "But seek first his kingdom and his righteousness, and all these things will be given to you as well" (Matt. 6:33). And, "Love your neighbor as yourself" (Matt. 22:39).

These are two of the simplest of God's directives in the Bible, yet at that moment I knew following them would change everything. Deep in my heart I felt God saying that if I sought Him and loved others, He'd handle the details. But to do what He was asking required a huge departure from the status quo.

If I helped start a crisis pregnancy center, I'd be stepping into an unfamiliar ministry and walking into a leadership role when the only job I'd ever held outside the home was as a McDonald's cashier. I felt completely unqualified and woefully unprepared. It came down to this: Did I believe God's Word enough to do what it said? Did I trust God to keep His promises?

Ephesians 3:16 says, "I pray that from his glorious, unlimited resources he will empower you with inner strength through his Spirit" (NLT). And that was my prayer too. I had to trust that if I did what God was asking, He would provide from His unlimited resources everything I needed, starting with inner strength.

In the days to come I wished I hadn't agreed to pray about Pastor Daniel's request, because it became clear that God wanted me to help start the center. The strength of my desire to follow His directives to *seek Him* and *love others* was at .01 percent, but the request was unmistakable.

The moment I chose to obey is the defining moment of my life.

People sometimes ask, "Why would God lead you in a new direction when you haven't obeyed the requests He's already given you?" Or as James 1:22 says, "Do not merely listen to the word, and so deceive yourselves. Do what it says." Obedience is always the first step to walking out God's directives. There is a difference, you see, between knowing what God's Word says and actually doing it. For me that difference came down to calling my pastor and telling him I was in. And then, in the days to come, taking one step after another and doing the work.

God wanted to use me, and the freedom I'd found in Him, to impact others. I was learning an important truth: our faith journey isn't about *our* dreams and ideas for how we can serve God, but about *His* dreams, plans, and desires for us, our community, and our world.

NOT JUST ABOUT US

Sometimes in the busyness of our Christian walk we forget that our ministry is not all about us and what we have to offer God. Many of us think it's up to us to figure out God's purposes for us. So we take personality inventories and spiritual gifts tests to identify our gifts and strengths, and to determine what kind of service matches our natural bent. God may use such things. The problem comes when we learn what we're good at and think that's all God will call us to do. And that's just not the case. Many people in history have shied away from God's call at first. Many biblical people too. Moses didn't think he could approach Pharaoh and request his people's freedom, but God called him to it anyway. Gideon and Deborah also shied away from God's call at first. At least I'm in good company.

Becoming a freelance author and a homeschooling mom came naturally to me because I write well and have a teacher's heart. They fit my bent. So did leading Bible studies. But the role of pregnancy center director did not play to my strengths. When I started the center, I felt far out of my comfort zone. I did things I had never done before: set agendas for meetings, recruited volunteers, and created and oversaw a budget. I planned training sessions and communicated with national organizations. I sat face-to-face with young moms in crisis and offered advice and hope in the midst of their fears. These tasks in no way lined up with what I felt were my spiritual gifts. Yet God had called me to do them. He knew there were women in my community who needed answers, help, and hope.

Most days in this role I felt unprepared and unsure. So, I sought advice from people I respected and trusted. I also prayed a lot. In the areas I felt weak, God strengthened me. In the areas I needed guidance and wisdom, He brought godly people who offered both. As I faced overwhelming challenges, God strengthened my skills and increased my faith. I wasn't a pregnancy center director because I'd dreamed about it and prepared for it, but because God needed me in that role for that season. God grew me through the ministry, and He grew the ministry through me.

After a few years, God brought another woman to take my place, and I was able to hand over a healthy, thriving organization and step down into the less-demanding volunteer role of teen mom support group coordinator.

Have you fallen into the trap, as so many other Christ-followers have, of believing God only calls us to do things that naturally match our personalities and spiritual gifts? Sometimes the things God asks us to do will seem like an easy fit, but other times they'll seem the opposite of what is most comfortable for us to do. And that's okay, because maybe the call has just as much to do with growing you into the person God wants you to be as it does about the specific work He wants you to accomplish.

Have you ever hesitated to step out and follow God in a certain area because it didn't seem like a perfect fit? When was the last time you read God's Word and promised yourself, "I'm going to do exactly what it says, no matter the cost"—and then followed through?

It seems to me that God does His best work through ill-fitted yet determined servants who willingly follow His directives. He used twelve men from humble, unexpected backgrounds to launch a movement that changed the world. He selected David, a shepherd boy, to become a king. He chose an unwed teenager to birth a Savior. And because each of those ordinary followers dared to trust God, God accomplished extraordinary things through them.

As God's children we can choose to follow Him or not. We are free to stay still, stay comfortable, and stay put. But our "freedom" may be our biggest weight, holding us back. "It is absolutely clear that God has called you to a free life," we read in Galatians 5:13–15. "Just make sure that you don't use this freedom as an excuse to do whatever you want to do and destroy your freedom. Rather, use your freedom to serve one another in love; that's how freedom grows. For everything we know about God's Word is summed up in a single sentence: Love others as you love yourself. That's an act of true freedom" (THE MESSAGE).

I could have refused to follow God's directive and gone on to live a simple, happy life. Yet what would it have cost me in my relationship with Jesus? A lot. And what would it have cost my community? I'm glad I don't have to find out. One step of obedience changed everything, including me.

WHEN WE SAY YES

When God asks us to step out in obedience, He doesn't ask us to journey alone. We are just a small part of His plan. He has been preparing the hearts of others too. When I stepped out, I discovered dozens of other men and women who wanted to make a difference in our community but didn't know how. Sometimes God just needs us to take the first step to get the ball rolling. And that's exactly how He used me.

Because I said yes, I experienced God growing Hope Pregnancy Center into a viable community resource that has helped and transformed lives. After seeing what God accomplished with my feeble efforts, it became easier to say yes the next time I felt His call. And the next. And the next.

Along the way, I discovered a new dream and purpose—to simply read God's Word, do what it says, and follow Jesus to places He was already at work in the world. Purpose, I've discovered, isn't something we need to figure out ahead of time. Instead it is something we often recognize in hindsight, as we follow Jesus one step at a time.

Now when I head to a lake on summer days and float on my back (which I still like to do) my mind doesn't wander and wonder what God has in store for me. Instead, I marvel at what God's already done. And I find joy in realizing His purposes for my future will be revealed as I take the next step.

FOR REFLECTION

1. When you were growing up, what were your dreams for your future? How would you have described your purpose in life? When in your life did it seem as if those dreams and purposes weren't going to come true?

2. Have you ever been disillusioned when it came to your dreams and purposes for your Christian walk? When have you felt as though you were doing everything for God but really missed connection with Him?

3. In what ways have you stepped out and followed God in obedience in the past? How did He show up as you did those things?

4. How do you think your life would change if you asked God to break your heart and change your dreams and purposes to encompass His clear directives in His Word?

ACTION STEPS

1. Write one thing you've felt God calling you to do but you've been afraid or unwilling to do because it's out of your comfort zone. What is God saying to you about it, even now?

2. Think about your story and how you discovered Christ's saving grace. Who in your community would be encouraged to hear that story? Set a time when you can share it with that person or group.

3. Think back and marvel over areas where God has shown up in your life. Thank Him for the purposes He still has ahead for you as He leads you in your next steps.

4. Pray and ask God to show you how to use your freedom in Him to impact another person or a group.

2

Loving and Serving from a Healed Heart

I was twenty-two years old when I attended my first writers' conference. I walked into the auditorium with my notebook and pens, hopes and expectations. No one suspected that I also carried a heavy load of heart-baggage. Not only had I had an abortion and endured a teen pregnancy, but my biological father had abandoned me, as had my baby's father. My heart was battered, torn, and weighed down. But on the outside I looked happy and excited. I didn't know how to deal with the pain, and so I buried it and did my best to ignore it. Before I could inspire, guide, or entertain anyone with my words, however, God had work to do in my heart.

It's not surprising that just as I ran from the pain and conflict in my life, I avoided it in my writing. I wanted to write sweet, Christian romances. The only problem was my plots lacked conflict. Without hardship and longing, my characters had little motivation and few internal struggles. (All of which are essential to good, heart-gripping novels.) How could I write deep and impactful things when I refused to unearth and face my own deep pain?

When I first became a Christian, I didn't understand my need for heart healing. Wasn't it enough that I'd given my life to Jesus? Yes, that was all that mattered in terms of my eternal salvation. But I couldn't give readers what I didn't have: faith that God wants to meet us in our deepest pain and do extraordinary things through our healed, albeit ordinary, hearts.

God also wants to heal us for ourselves, so we can experience peace. "When you're living in wholeness with Jesus and your heart is thriving, you can be unshakeable, living fully alive in each moment, taking risks, trusting your heart, fully aware of what you love, remaining yourself in every circumstance, and adoring God with every part of your being," writes Christa Black Gifford in her book *Heart Made Whole*. "However, if your heart remains broken, even as a Christian you will experience consistent separation between your heart, soul, mind, and spirit that keeps you from living in joyful connection with God and others."[1] These words describe exactly how I lived for years without realizing it. The wall of protection I'd built around my heart, not only kept out pain and sadness, it also kept out happiness and love.

Despite my loving family, I didn't feel love—neither theirs for me nor mine for them—and acted more out of duty than devotion. When I played peek-a-boo with my baby daughter, I smiled and laughed, but the joy didn't touch my heart. When my son fell and hurt himself, I ran to him and assisted him, but there was little compassion or concern. When I snuggled by my husband's side to watch a movie, I knew I should be happy and content, but I felt a numbness I couldn't shake.

Before I could open myself up to all the good things in my life, I had to open myself up to feeling all the pain, heartache, shame, and loss that came from my abortion and from being abandoned by men who were supposed to love me. It was easier to keep my emotions at arm's length than to feel the ache of loss.

I minimized the trauma I experienced from my dad by telling myself, *At least I wasn't one of those kids who had to split her time between her mom and dad's house.* And, *Maybe my biological dad wasn't that great of a person, so God removed him from the picture to protect me.* As for my old boyfriend, I told myself it was good that he abandoned my son and me because God brought John into our lives to be a husband and father.

But my rationalizations didn't relieve the pain. And the pain confirmed my childhood belief: I wasn't worth sticking around for. I felt unlovable and was too afraid of further rejection to share my weightiest sin and deepest regret with our Christian community. Only my parents, ex-boyfriend, and John knew about my abortion. I didn't even tell my closest friends. When the topic of abortion came up in church or Bible study, I sank deep into my seat, especially when people spoke doggedly against it. My stomach knotted up, and I was certain everyone within twenty feet of me heard the frantic pounding of my heart.

If they knew the truth and understood what I've done, they'd hate me. He wouldn't want to share a pew with me. She would turn and walk away in disgust.

Hiding from the truth protected me from the condemnation of others and from the ugliness of what I'd done, but it also blocked me from the beauty of life.

My shame began to heal the day I picked up the phone and signed up to attend a Bible study for women who'd had an abortion. My hands trembled as I drove to the church, yet walking into that room and seeing other women who'd made the same choice I had was a step of freedom. When I saw love and compassion in their eyes, a weight lifted off my shoulders. They saw me, knew what I'd done, and didn't despise me. After all, they'd faced the same pain.

That first night the leader asked us to share our stories. Telling these women the truth of my wrong choices opened my heart to healing. But deeper healing came when I began to believe God and the truth of His Word—the truth about forgiveness and how God sees me, my hurt, and my sin.

LIVING IN THE TRUTH OF GOD'S WORD

Since I was a young girl, I'd been told that God's Word was true. As a child I memorized Scripture verses so I could pick a prize from the treasure chest. And after I dedicated my life to Jesus at seventeen, those verses, seeds planted deep in my heart, became precious to me.

When I was a pregnant teen, God's Word often reminded me that Jesus had a good plan for my future. I clung to Jeremiah 29:11: "'For I know the plans I have for you,' declares the LORD, 'plans to prosper you and not to harm you, plans to give you hope and a future.'"

Years later, when I read my Bible as part of a post-abortion Bible study,[2] Jesus revealed new verses I needed to believe. One was 1 Peter 2:24: "He personally carried our sins in his body on the cross so that we can be dead to sin and live for what is right. By his wounds you are healed" (NLT).

Before I could embrace the hope and the future God had planned for me, I had to believe Jesus's death covered *all* my sins. As I studied the Bible with fresh eyes, I realized I'd turned over many of my sins to God, but I had kept the heaviest ones close to me. It was as though I wanted the rose *with* the thorns attached because I believed I deserved to be pierced.

Even though Jesus had forgiven me for my abortion, I'd never forgiven myself. This realization made me view my fifteen-year-old self differently. Instead of hatred and shame, I felt compassion for the girl I had been. I recognized my hunger to be loved and my frantic need to be held and cherished. I understood that I had tried to fill those open, deep chasms in the only way I knew—by seeking out affection—only to be hurt and abandoned again and again.

To step into all God had for me, I had to allow Jesus's love for me to penetrate my heart. "But he was pierced for our transgressions, he was crushed for our iniquities; the punishment that brought us peace was on him, and by his wounds we are healed," says Isaiah 53:5. I had to see myself as He sees me: whiter than snow (see Ps. 51:6–7). It was the only way I could embrace the good future He was preparing.

As I received His love, Jesus shattered the wall I'd built for protection, and I came alive. I was awakened not only to the love of the Holy Spirit, but also to the love of my husband and children, to the love of friends. I felt like a different person. When I believed God's Word and fully accepted His love and forgiveness, I was able to share this truth with others.

Here's the rub: before any of us can impact the world for good or share God's good news, we need to understand—and experience— the good news ourselves. We need to dwell in the truth of it.

I thank the Lord my earliest attempts at writing never made it to print. The themes in my fiction were empty and artificial, the characters flat and one dimensional. I wrote nonfiction from a place of "this sounds good" instead of "this is God's truth I know deep in my heart." Now as I write, I often include my story of pain, shame, healing, hope, and freedom. I've shared it in books, on radio broadcasts, on television, and in numerous blogs. I've told it one-on-one in the ministries I serve. My pain, once it was covered in God's love, became the very thing that gave my life and ministry vibrancy, richness, and meaning.

WHAT TO DO WITH YOUR DISTRESS

Maybe abortion isn't part of your story, but if you are like many of the women I meet, something you've done—or perhaps something done to you—prevents you from deeply experiencing God's unconditional love and forgiveness. "God's passion is to rig the world so that we are compelled to deal with whatever blocks us from being like His glorious Son," wrote Dan Allender.[3] Jesus allowed me to carry my pain until I reached the place where dealing with it was easier than hauling it around. Have you arrived at that place?

Nowhere in the Bible does God say He wants us to carry the pain of our sin to punish us; instead He wants our pain to draw us to Him. I love how the *The Message* expresses this truth:

> Now I'm glad—not that you were upset, but that you were jarred into turning things around. You let the distress bring you to God, not drive you from him. The result was all gain, no loss.
>
> Distress that drives us to God does that. It turns us around. It gets us back in the way of salvation. We never regret that kind of pain. But those who let distress drive them away from God are full of regrets, end up on a deathbed of regrets.
>
> And now, isn't it wonderful all the ways in which this distress has goaded you closer to God? You're more alive, more concerned, more sensitive, more reverent, more human, more passionate, more responsible. Looked at from any angle, you've come out of this with purity of heart. (2 Cor. 7:9–13)

When I believed what Scriptures such as this said about my sin and hurt, I asked God to come near, knowing that only He could heal all those bruised and broken places. As Jesus's presence softened my heart, His living water seeped in and brought new life. As I let Him tear down the wall around my heart, His love took root, grew, and spread, allowing me truth and joy to share with others through my life, my work, and my words.

Please don't keep hiding your pain and shame for fear of what others will think. Don't cling to the ache because you feel you deserve to suffer. Jesus longs for each of us to allow our pain to draw us to Him. He wants us to believe and trust *all* His words in the Bible. When we continue to carry the burden of our sin we say what Jesus did on the cross wasn't good enough. God's Word reminds us Jesus died for *all* our sins—not just the ones we don't think were that bad—and His healing is available for *every part* of our hearts.

Once I felt the freedom this brings, and my burden lifted, my gratitude was strong. I wanted to do everything I could to help others experience the same. Six months after my own healing I helped lead a Bible study just like the one I'd attended. David's prayer became my own: "LORD my God, I called to you for help, and you healed me.... Weeping may stay for the night, but rejoicing comes in the morning" (Ps. 30:2, 5).

WHOLENESS NOT PERFECTION

Anytime you want to move forward in a relationship or calling, don't be surprised if Jesus wants to accomplish a deeper level of healing in you first. Then again, don't use "God is still healing me" as an excuse to procrastinate from stepping out to serve others. Sometimes we must pause and allow Jesus to speak to us about the pain in our hearts before we proceed, and other times we need to journey forward before the healing is complete. Wholeness doesn't mean perfection.

That said, even after I found healing from my abandonment and abortion, Jesus often used pauses in my life. However, as you'll see in the pages to come, for me God's deeper work nearly always happened before each new step He asked me to take. God knows what's to come, and He knows with each new faith step we'll have plenty of external challenges without having to battle internal struggles too.

We will never be perfect while we are on this earth. And we can't wait until we "arrive" to serve Him, because we will never reach that place. Instead, we are to lean on Jesus with every step, knowing He will fill in the gaps with His goodness and grace.

Perhaps my story will help you discover even more completely the grace, peace, and forgiveness of Jesus, but I hope this message doesn't stop there. I hope *your* healing leads you to share your story with even one person. True freedom lightens our steps and makes a way into the purpose God intended for us from the beginning. It's from a healed heart that we can truly love and serve.

FOR REFLECTION

1. In what way has your broken heart, even as a Christian, kept you from living in joyful connection with God and others?

2. Often we hide our sins for self-protection. How does hiding make you feel? What might Jesus be asking you to do instead of hiding?

3. What Scripture verses do you struggle to believe? Why do you think they are harder to trust than others?

4. Reflect on a time when you asked God to forgive you for something, and you truly embraced His forgiveness. How did living in His forgiveness change how you felt inside?

ACTION STEPS

1. Do you have a wall around your heart? Talk with Jesus about the pain, shame, or regret that erected the wall there.

2. Even though you've asked God to forgive you, do you struggle to forgive yourself for something you did or was done to you? Prayerfully look back on that time in your life and ask Jesus to help you view yourself and your mistakes through eyes of compassion.

3. Are you using your shortcomings as an excuse for not reaching out to others? Pray and ask Jesus to help you step out in wholeness, even though you'll never reach perfection.

3

Creating White Space, Crafting Purpose

I have a hard time sitting still. I blame my inability to rest, in part, on my mother and grandmother, who were dogged about housework. When I was growing up, the laundry was always caught up, the ironing was always done, and the house was always clean. Well, except for my room. It was the messiest one in the house, and when it got bad enough my mom would pick up for me.

Mother and Grandmother's diligence impacted me, and eventually I believed what they modeled: cleanliness is next to godliness. One didn't rest until the work was done. Of course, a woman's work is never done! It's easy to stay busy, fill our schedules, and never stop to rest. But what does this do to our souls? For me, staying busy offers an escape from all that's happening on the inside—worries, anxieties, and fears.

I suspect this is one reason why for many years I struggled to sit still before God. My morning routine involved Bible reading and prayer, but that quiet time was more about the activity than the relationship. Even then I was busy "doing." I focused on Bible study homework, prayed through a prayer list, and read through a yearly Bible reading plan. Sometimes my quiet time turned into work time when a Scripture verse sparked an idea for a devotional article or blog.

Like everything else, "time with God" was something to mark off my to-do list. My soul was yet another item that "needed to be fixed." The thing is, the spiritual life doesn't work that way. You and I can't become better people by finding the right recipe for prayer or checking off a list of spiritual disciplines. We can't manufacture understanding or compassion for others by willpower. We can't produce the fruit of the Spirit by rolling up our sleeves. We best experience love, joy, peace, patience, kindness, goodness, faithfulness, gentleness, and self-control when we grant the Holy Spirit access to every part of our hearts. If anything should be on our to-do list it's this: connect with Jesus. Fall deeper in love with Him.

DRIVEN TO PROVE MYSELF

I now realize life isn't just about what I can get done. But it took me years longer than it should have to learn this lesson. Why? Because I allowed no white space—empty space—on my calendar or in my heart. I kept busy because I believed what I chose to do or not do with my time was up to me. And because deep down I felt insecure.

I felt I had to prove my value and worth to the people who knew me during my teenage years. Even after John and I moved a thousand miles from our small hometown, an inner voice urged me on: "I'll prove to *them* I didn't make a mistake by becoming a teen mom. I'll show *them* young moms can be good moms and can go on to do great things." Who was *them*? Simply the people I felt I'd disappointed: classmates, teachers, and friends.

I felt I had to prove to my mom I was a good housekeeper. When I was young and had a messy room, she'd always tell me, "I'd hate to see what your house will look like when you're an adult." So, as an adult, those words echoed in my head any time dishes filled the sink or dirty clothes littered the laundry room floor.

I also felt driven to prove myself to my biological father. I didn't know anything but his name, yet with the Internet I knew that could change. I suspected if I typed his name in a search engine, I could find him. Yet for years I didn't allow myself to do that. Why? Because I had something to prove to him too—that I was worthy to be his daughter. I told myself I had to reach two goals before I looked for my father: lose weight (and become super-model thin) and get a book published. Rejection seemed less likely if I was both beautiful and successful. I never admitted this, of course, but these feelings of insecurity kept me pushing forward and wouldn't allow me to rest.

THE DIFFICULTY OF BEING STILL

During this time of striving and constantly trying to prove myself, God brought a verse to mind. I saw it in books. I heard it in sermons. I received it cross-stitched on a small wall hanging from my step-mom: "Be still, and know that I am God" (Ps. 46:10).

I put the wall hanging in my bathroom as a reminder that I needed to pause, but I couldn't force myself to actually be quiet before God. After all, what if I allowed myself to be still, to be vulnerable, and I didn't measure up? I believed the lie that *what I did* mattered more than *who I was* … even to my heavenly Father.

Instead I stayed busy and ignored the ache in my soul. I made my Bible reading time something to accomplish. If people needed help at church or a babysitter or for some task to be done, they could count on me. After all, if I wasn't doing all these wonderful things, how would people see me? What would my house look like? How would my kids turn out?

My full calendar made me feel accomplished; it made me look important, needed, valuable. But the cost was great. I was stressed. I was overwhelmed. I was tired all the time. My shoulders grew weary from the high level of expectations, especially my own.

I'm not the only one who struggles with doing too much. Lately, I've noticed we've changed our vocabulary in this country. When someone asks how we're doing, instead of answering, "Fine," we say, "Busy." Yet if we don't have time for a bubble bath, then we often don't have time for God.

CREATING WHITE SPACE

My busyness and full calendar became too much. John noticed things weren't right and suggested I cut back. I didn't listen. At least not at first.

One evening he arrived home from work and found I'd reached my breaking point. It was 6 o'clock, and I hadn't started dinner.

The kids were fighting, and I'd been in a bad mood most of the day because I was exhausted. I'd just gotten home from grocery shopping and was still lugging the bags in from the car. When John walked into the kitchen, I dropped my load. As the groceries tumbled to the floor, tears tumbled from my eyes.

"I can't do this," I said with trembling lips. "I feel as if I'm never home. We're running from place to place, and the kids are fighting all the time. I'm tired, and I just don't want to do any of it anymore!"

John could have said, "I told you so," but he didn't. His gaze spoke love and compassion. "That's it," he said. "After dinner we're going over your schedule. You can't keep up this pace."

I was happy for us to go over my schedule. I wanted John to see *all* I did, and maybe have a little more compassion. Also, I was pretty sure there wasn't much to give up. Everything *felt* important. Everything *made me feel* important.

After dinner John sat down with me and asked some questions:

- What are the most important things in your life?
- What things do you really value?
- What things are you doing because you didn't want to say no?
- What things do you wish you could give up but feel like you can't because doing so would be backing out on a commitment?
- What activities are the kids involved in that sounded like a good idea at first but are not really working?

As we talked, John pointed out three things. First, we didn't have to do everything in this one season of life. Second, if something wasn't working, we didn't have to keep doing it. And third, we couldn't do what God asked us to do (the true desires of our hearts) if so many other things filled our minds, attentions, and schedules.

These insights apply to each of us. We can walk out Scripture's mandates only if we make room for God to work in our hearts and lives. I needed to be still and know that He is God (see Ps. 46:10) so I could hear His still, small voice and better understand *His* purposes for me.

John helped me clear out the clutter by suggesting I list everything I did in a week. Once I did that, we numbered each item from one to four, in order of importance. Here's how we determined the level of importance:

1. Things I *had* to do. (Things that were non-negotiable: feed children, get them dressed, homeschooling/homework, writing assignments, Bible study, and prayer.)
2. Things I *should* do. (Things that were ideal to do, but could occasionally be skipped, or someone could help with: laundry, cook dinner, bathe my kids, serve others.)
3. Things I w*anted* to do. (Things I enjoyed doing and what helped me: Bible study group, exercise class, coffee with a friend, a child's favorite sport or activity.)

4. Things I *didn't need* to do. (Things done out of duty
   or guilt or to look good: volunteering because I
   couldn't say no, extracurricular activities, things
   I thought made me a good mom.)

Then John asked me to do something drastic:

1. Cut out all the fours—the things I was doing in
   order to look good or out of guilt.
2. Limit the threes, realizing there would be
   different seasons in life when I could do other
   things I wanted to do.
3. Take a moment to appreciate the white space
   created when I cut these things from my schedule.
4. Identify family goals and create habits around
   those goals.

By the end of the night I agreed to John's requests. I decided
to stop volunteering to clean the church and cook for our church's
Wednesday night supper. I stepped down from a community Bible
study because it wasn't the right season for it. We took our daughter
out of ballet and our son out of T-ball, knowing they didn't like
these activities anyway. I also promised not to say yes to any commitment unless I talked to John about it first. Not that I needed his
permission; I just needed his help in accurately gauging the time and
commitment required. And do you know what? When I looked at
my calendar at the end of the night, I saw white space on it!

In the weeks and months that followed, this breathing room became my saving grace. I was happy not to be running so much. I enjoyed not being stressed or frantic. And with some of the hours I freed up in my day, I opened myself up to God. I read my Bible and prayed—not to check something off my list but to connect with Him.

During this period Jesus led me to verses that showed me I had nothing to prove. One of them was Zephaniah 3:17: "God is with you, the Mighty Warrior who saves. He will take great delight in you, in his love he will no longer rebuke you, but will rejoice over you with singing."

In the months and years that followed, I learned that being quieted with God's love was a beautiful thing, and it started with being still.

As I sat before Jesus, He not only revealed His good purposes for me, He also began showing me His purposes for our family.

CRAFTING A FAMILY OF PURPOSE

In the process of trimming our commitments, John and I also set up a framework of priorities for our family. Identifying our priorities and eliminating what didn't fit helped us establish a family life filled with meaning and purpose, one that included the space to follow God wherever He would lead.

Stated another way, we *formed* (created our family value system and framework) before we *filled* (added things into our lives). The idea of forming before filling isn't something we came up with on our own. It came from the first pages of the Bible. In the first three days

of creation, God "formed." He established supportive systems neces-
sary for life and humankind's existence. He created the heavens and
the earth. He separated the waters from the land. He made the stars
and sun. He built the framework that would sustain His creation.

The last three days, God "filled." He filled His created world
with plants, flowers, animals, and humankind. The process unfolded
like this:

> Formed: Day One—Created light; formed heavens
> and earth
> Filled: Day Four—Filled with sun, moon, and stars
> Formed: Day Two—Separated water and sky
> Filled: Day Five—Filled with fish and birds
> Formed: Day Three—Formed land and vegetation
> Filled: Day Six—Filled with animals and man

The problem comes when we *fill* our weekly and monthly schedules before we build a structure for them. We make decisions out of
emotions or desires without contemplating their impact on us. But
as I've experienced, this never works. Few good things ever happen
by accident.

A schedule with white space isn't the goal, of course. A family
life flourishing with meaning and purpose is the goal. As I've learned
in many areas of my life, if you want something good to happen, it's
important to build some structure around it.

As John and I considered the type of people we wanted to be, and
the type of children we wanted to raise, six priorities rose to the top.

1. ATTENDING CHURCH

For us church attendance has never been optional. God's Word is clear on this. We read in Hebrews 10:25: "And let us not neglect our meeting together, as some people do, but encourage one another, especially now that the day of his return is drawing near" (NLT).

Attending church is important for our family. We are happy to set aside time to honor the Lord and gather with other believers. It's important to hear God's Word preached and to come together in corporate worship. Some of our very best friends have been those we've attended church with. These people have not only been friends to John and me, but friends and role models for our children as they've grown older. Every family needs this type of accountability and support system.

2. SERVING OTHERS TOGETHER (WITHIN OUR CHURCH AND BEYOND)

John and I wanted our kids to learn how to serve, even from a young age. When I launched Hope Pregnancy Center, they helped remodel our ministry building by pulling up carpet and picking up trash. They folded baby clothes and stacked diapers. My daughter Leslie even babysat for our teen mom support group. At first I felt guilty. Other kids were outside playing or hanging out with friends, but I soon discovered that our kids were proud of their efforts, and it became easier for them to serve in other ways.

Our kids were also involved with the children's ministry John and I and our best friends started in our church. We acted out Bible stories and application skits, and they joined in, finding themselves in all types of interesting costumes during the week. Our three oldest children grew up serving others. They are now adults. Our oldest sons serve in children's church. Our oldest daughter is a missionary and active in her local church in the Czech Republic where she lives. They've become so comfortable with serving it's a natural part of who they are.

3. READING THE BIBLE AND PRAYING TOGETHER

Every school day morning we read from the Bible and a devotional book, and then pray together. We do this first thing. I want to show my kids that reading the Bible is always a priority.

John and I also read the Bible and pray with each other in the mornings. We don't succeed every day, but we do it most days. Our youngest children are often awake at that time, and though they know they can't interrupt, they love watching us. Sometimes when I open my eyes after praying I find three little kids sitting at our feet, listening to every word. It's especially sweet when later, during their prayer time, I hear my words repeated as they pray for family members and concerns. Although having kids watch me while I pray sometimes feels awkward, I know it's important. It models for them what a healthy spiritual life can look like.

4. EATING FAMILY DINNER TOGETHER

John and I decided our kids knowing each other and us was important, as was face-to-face connection while eating a meal around the table. During family dinners we talk about our day and enjoy the conversation. We expect our kids to help out with these meals. Some of them help cook dinner, others set the table. Afterward our kids help clear the table and put away food, unload and load the dishwasher, wash the pots and pans, wipe down the counters, and sweep the floor. To us, the cleanup routine is just as important as the dinner conversation. Together all of these activities teach our children what being part of a family is all about.

5. READING AT BEDTIME TOGETHER

One of my favorite times of the day is when I get the little kids settled in at night and it's time to read. We turn off all electronics, the kids get ready for bed, and then we sit down together. Our adult kids still look back on reading time with fondness. We've never regretted the time we've spent together within the pages of a book.

6. SUPPORTING EVERYONE'S TALENTS AND ACTIVITIES TOGETHER

Whenever one of our children is involved in an activity, we show up as a family to support them. This has included attending football games to watch our daughter in the marching band or going to state-wide basketball games for our son. We want our children to know they are uniquely special and their whole family is cheering them on.

These priorities led to habits that fostered a more focused and settled spirit as a family. Even though we have a large family, we established patterns to our days and weeks. The time we spend together makes us closer. Our priorities guide us when it comes to knowing what to say yes to and what to say no to. They help us determine what's best for *all of us*, not just for one person in the family. Our choices have directed us to a quieter life, even as we've continued to add to our family through adoption.

Not too long after John and I went through the calendar-clearing exercises, I came across another verse that confirmed we were on the right track. Ecclesiastes 4:6 says, "Better is a handful of quietness than two hands full of toil and a striving after wind" (ESV). Clearing my calendar and establishing family priorities didn't just bring calm to my day, it also brought peace to my soul, making room for God to work. As Colossians 3:15 says, "Let the peace of Christ rule in your hearts."

In the months that followed, whenever I was tempted to default and add on "just one more thing" I'd remind myself that adding more was just chasing the wind. As my soul settled and I stopped trying to prove myself, I started asking God to show me His heart, to direct my path, and to guide my steps. I told Him I wanted *His purpose* for my life—our lives, not just mine. And I discovered God had been waiting for us to join His work all along.

THE PATHS GOD HAS PREPARED FOR US

Once I created white space and had a framework to guide family decisions, my mind became less cluttered, my days less frantic, and my heart more open to God's will.

His gentle leading started in small ways. One day when I was praying for Him to show me someone I could reach out to, He brought my husband's coworker to mind. John had been suggesting for months that we invite this family over for dinner. Now I followed this gentle nudge I knew was from the Holy Spirit.

Skyler and Tara came to dinner, and before long we jumped into a deep, spiritual conversation. They were looking for a church home after years of letting that priority slip from their lives, so John and I invited them to our church. The next week they not only started attending our church, they joined a Bible study with us. My heart filled with joy. God confirmed how *He could work* if I opened my heart and schedule to Him.

What about you? Does peace even in the midst of a full life sound like something you are searching for, but it seems unattainable? Do you question if it's even possible to allow for God to determine your steps in today's busy world? If so, you're on the journey I, and many of my friends, have been on.

"There are good things I'm doing, but I often wonder if they are the best things," my friend Jen confessed. I feel that way sometimes; maybe you do too. But as we seek to live out God's purposes, we learn to trust Him to lead us to those "best things."

My friend Ann attests to this. She told me, "I believe God will always work His purposes for me, because I am not 'big' enough to mess up His plans. He keeps me in His plan by nudging me when I start to veer. He uses the 'too busy' feeling to help me focus on what's important to keep our relationship maintained—to keep me open to when He's redirecting me."

Like Ann, I'm thankful God redirects me with inner nudges when I'm busy doing things that don't fit with His purposes for me or for our family. When I create white space on the calendar, and focus on my established priorities, God shows up. And that's when I discover His invitations for me to join Him in His work.

JOINING GOD

It was not long after John and I completed these exercises, recentering our lives, that Pastor Daniel approached me about helping start Hope Pregnancy Center. Yes, dedicating time to that pursuit added to my schedule, but I stepped forward in faith, confident this was work in the community God wanted to do—work He wanted to involve me in. But I was only able to follow His leading because I'd cut so many other things from my schedule and had identified my priorities.

What am I missing out on by following Jesus's purposes? Being the look-good-on-the-outside soccer mom, active homeschool mom, and you-can-count-on-me church volunteer. What have I discovered instead? Peace, joy, and purpose.

Jesus wants to accomplish things in this world, and He will not leave those things undone. Will we join Him in accomplishing His purposes? Few good things ever happen by accident. We must decide who we want to be, and who we want our children to be, and then create the habits that will help us grow into those types of people.

I love *The Message* translation of the story of the two men who built their homes on different foundations:

> These words I speak to you are not incidental additions to your life, homeowner improvements to your standard of living. They are foundational words, words to build a life on. If you work

these words into your life, you are like a smart carpenter who built his house on solid rock. Rain poured down, the river flooded, a tornado hit—but nothing moved that house. It was fixed to the rock.

But if you just use my words in Bible studies and don't work them into your life, you are like a stupid carpenter who built his house on the sandy beach. When a storm rolled in and the waves came up, it collapsed like a house of cards. (Matt. 7:24–27)

I have no doubt that if John hadn't stopped me and forced me to create some white space and consider our family priorities and foundation, at least my part of the foundation would have been built on sand. You can only be blown in so many different directions for so long without collapsing like a house of cards.

"Blessed are the single-hearted, for they shall enjoy much peace," wrote Amy Carmichael. "If you refuse to be hurried and pressed, if you stay your soul on God, nothing can keep you from that clearness of spirit which is life and peace. In that stillness you will know what His will is."[1]

FOR REFLECTION

1. In what ways have you considered your busy schedule a badge of honor?

2. What causes you to add activities to your schedule? For example: Worry about what others will think? Fear you're not doing enough? Eagerness to do more for God? Feelings of inadequacy and a desire to prove yourself? Something else?

3. What activities/commitments do you wish you could give up but are afraid to back out of? How would you feel if those things weren't on your schedule?

4. Name one thing God has asked you to join Him in but you have been unable to do because you haven't had the time and space? What could you cut to make adding this possible?

ACTION STEPS

1. Write out all you do in a week. Prioritize your tasks from one to four. Consider cutting all the fours and some of the threes.

2. Set up time to be still before God without an agenda. Simply open your Bible and desire to connect with Him.

3. Identify your priorities for your family. If you're married, talk over your priorities with your spouse. What's most important? Consider how to rearrange your family's schedule to fit those priorities.

4

Heaven over My Shoulder

Growing up, I knew my grandfather loved me. I have wonderful memories of things we did together. Sometimes he gave me pony rides on his knee. Other times we sat side-by-side on the couch, cracking walnuts together. (I ate more than I put into the bowl!) Sometimes when we drove to town he'd let me sit on his lap and I'd steer his truck. I was a Papa's girl, without a doubt.

Papa was eighty-two years old when the diagnosis of bladder cancer came. He told us he'd had a good life, and he didn't want to go through chemo treatments. Instead, he and my grandma moved in with our family, and I helped care for him during his last months on earth.

Those five months changed me. God's directive I'd learned as a child in Sunday school became a neon sign that flashed and buzzed through every crevice of my soul: "Do not lay up for yourselves treasures on earth, where moth and rust destroy and where thieves break in and steal, but lay up for yourselves treasures in heaven, where neither moth nor rust destroys and where thieves do not break in and steal. For where your treasure is, there your heart will be also" (Matt. 6:19–21 ESV).

I knew God would use this time with my grandfather to teach me the truths of His kingdom. He would lift my eyes away from the treasures on earth and direct them toward the true treasures in heaven.

A GLIMPSE OF HEAVEN

Month by month Papa grew weaker, but he maintained the same happy attitude. Sitting by his side, I read everything I could about heaven. Verses like Revelation 21:4 comforted me: "He will wipe every tear from their eyes, and there will be no more death or sorrow or crying or pain. All these things are gone forever" (NLT).

During the last week of Papa's life, the hospice nurse warned us the end was near. I sat next to him and read the Bible aloud. I prayed for him, both when he was awake and asleep. With each passing day the feeling in the room changed. A heavenly presence hung in the air, and sometimes I'd turn quickly, sure I'd glimpse an angel behind me. Heaven had touched earth and that room was the vertex. Even as my grandfather's body weakened, his spirit strengthened, preparing to burst from its earthly shell.

A few days before he died, my grandfather glimpsed heaven and gave a full report. I was out of the room, but my grandmother sat by his side. She was singing and praying when my grandfather interrupted her.

"Dear, do you smell that?" he asked. "It's the most wonderful aroma."

Then he pointed outside the window. "Look at those birds. Have you ever seen such beautiful birds?" As he stared ahead, Papa's eyebrows lifted and he peered closer. "Oh, do you see that lion? If I were an artist I would love to paint that lion."

Then the image of the lion apparently faded and a new vision appeared. With this one, Papa lifted his hands and started weeping, praising and worshipping Jesus. My grandma rushed to get me, and soon we were worshipping with him. Only afterward did my grandfather explain what he had seen. As he stared at the tree outside the bedroom window, the tree transformed into a cross and he witnessed Jesus hanging from it. Then Jesus, in all His glory, stepped forward and stretched out His arms to my grandfather.

My grandfather's experience reminded me of Revelation 5:5: "But one of the twenty-four elders said to me, 'Stop weeping! Look, the Lion of the tribe of Judah, the heir to David's throne, has won the victory. He is worthy to open the scroll and its seven seals'" (NLT).

During his last conscious moments, Papa blew a kiss at me and waved. I will always cherish that memory. It was his final good-bye.

Walking with my grandfather as he transitioned from earthly to eternal life showed me how thin the veil is between heaven and earth. When death stopped at our home, eternity ripped open, allowing a saint to step into the place his Savior had been preparing for him.

My grandfather was great in my eyes, but to the world he was no one important. One of eleven children, he was raised on a farm in Kansas, and his family moved to California during the Dust Bowl. He served in World War II, married a shy waitress, and raised three girls. He worked in a door factory until he retired, and then he tended a small garden behind his mobile home. He became a Christian later in life and lived a simple faith. But according to his Savior, a simple faith was all that was needed.

Jesus gives us an eternity with Him in exchange for a submissive heart that dares to trust and believe His life, death, and resurrection make us right before God. Papa probably made millions of decisions throughout his life, but when it came down to that chilly day in March, as he breathed his last breath, only one of those decisions mattered—he had chosen Jesus to be his Lord.

LONGING FOR HEAVEN

If you haven't faced the death of someone you love dearly, no words can describe the pain. My heart ached, and I questioned how the world could keep spinning. After my grandfather's death it seemed wrong people were still grocery shopping and going on vacation. I wanted the world to stop. I wanted people to acknowledge that *my world* would never be the same without my grandfather in it. But at the same time I experienced a beautiful grace.

Jerry Sittser, who witnessed his wife, mother, and daughter die in a tragic car accident, testifies to the kind of grace that comes through the death of those we love:

> Gifts of grace come to all of us. But we must be ready to see and willing to receive these gifts. It will require a kind of sacrifice, the sacrifice of believing that, however painful our losses, life can still

be good—good in a different way than before, but
nevertheless good. I will never recover from my loss
and I will never get over missing the ones I lost. But
I still cherish life.... I will always want the ones I
lost back again. I long for them with all my soul.
But I still celebrate the life I have found because
they are gone. I have lost, but I have also gained. I
lost the world I loved, but I gained a deeper awareness of grace. That grace has enabled me to clarify
my purpose in life and rediscover the wonder of the
present moment.[1]

My experience was similar. After Papa's death, I wanted heaven
like I'd never wanted it before. At the same time, I no longer wanted
to go through life blindly. During those five months I took a crash
course on what really mattered. I now noticed the little things. The
present moments of every day became full of wonder.

FROM EARTHLY PURSUITS TO HEAVENLY ONES

Before my grandfather's illness, I lived as if this earth is all there
is. I filled my closet with clothes. I planned the perfect vacations.
I paged through *Good Housekeeping* magazines, discontented with
our two-thousand-square-foot house. I eyed nice SUVs while driving
my minivan. I bought into the lie that I needed to do more and
get more so I could be happier. The grace given to me through my
grandfather's passing was the ability to see my life in light of eternity.

"Command those who are rich in this present world not to be arrogant nor to put their hope in wealth, which is so uncertain, but to put their hope in God, who richly provides us with everything for our enjoyment," we read in 1 Timothy 6:17. "Command them to do good, to be rich in good deeds, and to be generous and willing to share. In this way they will lay up treasure for themselves as a firm foundation for the coming age, so that they may take hold of the life that is truly life" (vv. 18–19).

This directive contains great wisdom, as it turns the world's understanding of wealth on its head. True wealth is being rich in good deeds. True treasure is yet to come.

Have you discovered "the life that is truly life"? Do you often lift your eyes toward eternity instead of the next big purchase? Or is the opposite true? Are you so busy buying, cleaning, and organizing your earthly treasures you don't have time to even think about your heavenly ones, let alone share them? Is your time so occupied with helping your kids earn good grades, become star athletes, or build their social skills that you haven't focused on nurturing their eternal souls?

We often fill our Instagram and Facebook feeds with pictures of our stuff while ignoring our neighbor, who lives forty feet away, has never accepted Christ, has no hope in heaven, and believes that her treasures on earth are all there is.

Though we claim to follow Jesus, we walk through life as if this is it. As though we must grasp all the pleasures we can before it's too late. We surround ourselves with comfort because it's a harsh world out there. We raise our kids in a bubble, attempting to shield them from pain. We don't look any different from the world around us, probably because we don't feel very different inside. We strive for the American dream while loving Jesus a little on the side.

My heart aches knowing this, and I often wonder what my life would look like today if I hadn't had that brush with eternity. Would I have traveled to the other side of the world to share the gospel? Would I have attended an inner-city church and reached out to the community? Would John and I have adopted seven kids? I'm not sure we would have done any of it.

Although I'd been a Christian for years, experiencing my grandfather's transition from earth to heaven sparked a longing for heaven for the first time. I also gained a burden for those who didn't know Jesus, who have no hope of heaven. Billions of people out there are facing death without the joy we experienced when Papa's eternal soul entered its eternal home.

As I walked with my grandfather through the shadow of death, my mind and heart shifted focus from earthly pursuits to eternal ones. All the things I'd been obsessed about didn't matter.

Did it matter, in light of eternity, if my house was neatly decorated or clean all the time?

Did it matter, in light of eternity, how many articles I published in a month or if I ever landed a book contract?

Did it matter, in light of eternity, if I ever lost that thirty extra pounds that didn't seem to budge?

For so many years, my actions showed I cared more about others' approval of me than God's. I scoured the house from top to bottom before friends came over, instead of snuggling with my kids or pausing to listen to my husband tell me about his day. I was horrified when one of my kids acted up in public because it made me look bad, instead of seeing those times as opportunities to guide and train my kids. When I taught a Bible study or encouraged a hurting woman, I came home and evaluated *my* performance. Could I have done something better? Could I have said or done anything to make a greater impact?

Are you living that same way?

We can be so concerned with how we look to others (or how our house, marriage, or kids look), that we ignore how we look to God. How do you think God feels and reacts when He watches our vain pursuits? We spend more time doing things *right* rather than being a *light* to this dark and hurting world.

Walking with my grandfather as he stepped into eternity reminded me that our Christian walk isn't about attaining some perfect ideal; it's about knowing Jesus—-and yet so many people do not know Him and have no hope of eternity with our Savior. I began to pray, *Lord, I can't change the world, but will You help me to reach just one person?*

Up until then, I wasn't much concerned with sharing Christ with unbelievers. Somehow, I'd ignored all the Scriptures about laying up treasures in heaven and giving others the hope of eternity simply because I'd been too focused on so many other things. I had surrounded myself almost exclusively with Christians, to the point there was no place for unbelievers in my life, but I knew that had to change. I knew I needed to leave my comfort zone and move toward those who never would naturally gravitate toward me, or to the Lord. So when Pastor Daniel asked me to help start Hope Pregnancy Center, I said yes.

GIVING ETERNITY TO JUST ONE PERSON

A young woman walked into the center with two pigtails situated at the top of her head. Kayleigh was fifteen but looked twelve. During our first teen mom support group meeting she told me she and her boyfriend were going to have their own place soon. She said they had been trying to raise their daughter while couch surfing and staying with different family members on alternating days.

Kayleigh didn't have any worries about eternity; she was just trying to survive the next day. I recognized a desperation in her eyes I somehow couldn't relate to. I later found out its cause. Her stepfather had sexually abused her for years. She'd believed if she got pregnant she could create her own family and escape the hell-hole she lived in.

She started attending the support group at the center, but initially I wondered why she came. She had a rude attitude and a hard heart. I was certain she wasn't listening to a word I said. I talked about Jesus, and all He had to offer her in this life and the next, and instead of acknowledging my message she'd slip outside for a smoke.

Kayleigh attended our meetings for three years, and then became pregnant again. I was frustrated. Why was I pouring all my time into these young women, telling them about Jesus and eternity? It didn't seem to matter at all.

Then a miracle touched earth. Heaven glanced down on a broken heart. When her second baby was only a few months old, Kayleigh married her boyfriend and accepted Christ. Overnight she was a new person. She connected with a church body, grew in her faith, and began to share Jesus with others.

As Kayleigh has journeyed with Jesus, allowing Him into the pain and shame of her past, He has healed the broken pieces of her heart. Kayleigh is now one of my closest friends, and she continues to share Jesus with others, even as she's faced many more challenges.

This is what putting our treasure in eternity means: sharing our truest riches laid up in heaven and pointing others to eternal life with Jesus—even if we don't know what the outcome of our sharing will be. When we truly understand this treasure, we don't want to hoard it for ourselves.

Sharing Jesus all those years with dozens of young women who acted as if they couldn't care less wasn't easy. But it was worth it.

STAYING FOCUSED ON ETERNITY

Perhaps you are wondering how it is possible to stay focused on eternity in the midst of everyday life. I understand. Keeping our minds eternally focused is tricky. Life brings distractions: kids and loved ones get sick, chores need to be done, relationships need to be tended.

While it's not easy to focus on eternity, I find that when I look to Christ to help me, He does. I just have to ask. It's the same with anything else concerning His kingdom. God wants to do wonderful things through us; we just have to be willing. Hebrews 13:20–21 says, "Now may the God of peace … equip you with everything good for doing his will, and may he work in us what is pleasing to him, through Jesus Christ, to whom be glory for ever and ever. Amen." This equipping requires dying to self—to our wants, needs, and desires—and calls us to point others to the glory to come. Jesus's death made the way for us to come to Him, and our daily death to self allows Him to live in and through us.

One primary reason Jesus came to earth was to reveal that God has a master plan for righting everything that went wrong with sin and death, and to fulfill God's plan. That plan includes restoring everything back to its original glory, and God wants as many people as possible to live with Him forever in a glorious existence. Jesus willingly walked to the cross because He saw what sin was doing to us. And when I walk alongside Him, I see the pain and ache of sin too—and want to give the good news to those who don't share my hope of eternity.

This is not a new message. It's the message the first apostles shared. It's a message that has been spoken throughout history and throughout all people groups. I love this passage from *The Scottish Christian Herald* from 1841:

> Every day of our lives, indeed we ought to engage
> in such services. God ought to be worshipped, and
> his Word read in our families and in our closets,
> every day, without exception. We ought continually
> to bear about us a sense of the Divine presence, and
> in all our actions be influenced by the fear and the
> love of God, and respect to his glory; and it is only
> by daily and earnest prayer and supplication at a
> throne of grace, that we are enabled, in any degree,
> so to live.[2]

FOR REFLECTION

1. Have you ever walked alongside someone who was stepping into eternity? What did you learn from that experience?

2. What things on this earth distract you from the things of heaven?

3. How does having a tattered heart—one torn with love and compassion for people—make us more like Jesus?

4. What does it cost you to share your hope of heaven with another person? If you don't share, what does it cost them?

ACTION STEPS

1. Write a list of your current worries. How do they measure up in light of eternity? Pray and ask Jesus to give you an eternal focus.

2. Consider who God has brought into your life who needs to know about the hope of heaven. Pray for his or her heart to soften. Pray you don't get discouraged as you reach out to that person with love and care.

3. Prayerfully ask God to equip you with everything good to do His work. Ask Him for bravery to step out of your comfort zone.

5

A Story Worth Telling

Years ago Robin Jones Gunn, an author and friend of mine, came to Montana to speak at a women's retreat and to visit me. The night before the retreat Robin, our friend Joanna Weaver, and I were staying at a condo that offered a few special amenities. We decided it would be fun to soak in the hot tub as we gazed over the snowy landscape that surrounded us. The problem was, the hot tub didn't work. Joanna called the condo's owner, who was a friend, to notify her of the problem. Since it was already evening and a repairman couldn't come right away, the owner suggested we use the hot tub at her house instead.

"I'm out of town but I'll have the caretaker meet you to let you in," she told us.

The caretaker was waiting when we arrived, and we soon found out he'd brought his wife and son with him.

Robin and Joanna entered the home first, while I parked the car in the snow. As Robin entered, a darling strawberry-blond toddler trotted over to her, lifted his arms, and allowed her to scoop him up. His surprised young mom told Robin his name was Toby. He was eighteen months old and not usually that friendly with strangers.

That's the scene I entered into—Robin holding this adorable toddler. As I walked through the door, Toby's mother turned to me and froze. In a shaking voice she said, "It's you! You're the one who spoke at the luncheon two years ago."

I nodded, even though I wasn't sure what event she spoke about.

"Do you remember how you shared your story? You talked about being a teen mom and you prayed God would send you a Christian husband?"

I nodded.

"I don't know if you remember me telling you this after the luncheon, but I had just found out I was pregnant."

As I peered into her beautiful face, it all came back to me. This was the young woman who had stood to the side and waited until everyone had left. Her eyes had been wide and filled with fear.

"I remember you," I told her, reaching out my hand to take hers. "But I can't remember your name."

"Kelly," she reminded me. "I had an abortion scheduled just a few days later." Kelly gazed at Toby cuddled up in Robin's arms. "But after I heard your story and what you said about how God answered your prayers, I cancelled the appointment, and I prayed for a husband, just like you did."

Her smile widened, and tears formed in her eyes. "I always wanted to see you again so I could tell you God answered my prayers. He brought an amazing Christian guy into my life. Dave loves me, and he loves my son. We've been married for almost a year. When I think about what my life would be like right now if I hadn't heard your story and done what you suggested …"

By then we were all hugging and crying and hugging some more. Toby climbed into my arms and received my cuddles and kisses. It was such a beautiful moment. Light and hope seemed to fill the room.

That night, I thanked God for the miraculous encounter. And it was a miracle. It "just so happened" that our hot tub hadn't been working. It also "just so happened" that Dave brought Kelly and Toby along for the ride. The place Kelly and I met the second time was over a hundred miles away from where we met the first time. God used this encounter to remind me of the power of sharing our stories—not just the good parts but the pain and the heartache too.

THIS LITTLE LIGHT OF MINE

Kelly's story likely would have turned out differently if I'd kept my story to myself. I speak a lot these days, but I never wanted to be a professional speaker. My passion has always been writing! As a young Christian the only public speaking I'd done was for my college speech class, and each time I spoke in front of the group my knees quivered so much the teacher asked me if I needed to sit down.

Yet through the years as I studied God's Word and grew as a Christian, I knew the transformation in my heart wasn't something to keep to myself. God made His directive clear in His Word:

> You are the light of the world. A city on a hill
> cannot be hidden. Neither do people light a lamp
> and put it under a basket. Instead, they set it on

> a lampstand, and it gives light to everyone in the
> house. In the same way, let your light shine before
> men, that they may see your good deeds and glorify
> your Father in heaven. (Matt. 5:14–16 BSB)

I can't imagine any child who's grown up going to Sunday school not knowing the song that goes, "This little light of mine, I'm gonna to let it shine." My Sunday school teacher explained letting our light shine meant sharing Jesus with those we knew, so even though I was a timid child, I invited friends to vacation Bible school. I understood even then the world was a dark place that needed Jesus's light. And I liked hearing stories about how Jesus changed people. I remember listening to church members and visitors tell their testimonies about how God had saved them from drugs, sex, and cults. (It was the early 1980s after all.) I can't remember many sermons I heard growing up, but I do remember when people talked about how God saved them, changed them, and was now using them.

But in the early years after I became a Christian I resisted telling others about what Jesus had done for me. My sin was so dark. The last thing I wanted to tell people was that I'd had two teen pregnancies and an abortion. Yet I couldn't share about my soul's transformation without revealing where I'd been and what I'd done.

When I finally started telling my story, I spoke in smaller settings, like the teen mom support group. Whenever people suggested I share it with larger groups I brushed their comments aside. When Pastor Daniel asked me to speak in front of the church I told him I'd think about it. Still, God wouldn't let me shake the feeling that I should do it.

In my daily Bible reading, I kept running across passages like this: "For once you were full of darkness, but now you have light from the Lord. So live as people of light!" (Eph. 5:8 NLT). It wasn't a suggestion, but a command. To live as a person of light was to spread the good news of Jesus—the light—through the world.

"This little light of mine, I'm going to let it shine," my children would sing, piercing my soul. The conviction grew that God was opening a door for me to share my story in a wider context, and I needed to walk through it.

Finally one spring day as the Holy Spirit was nudging me about this during my quiet time, I landed on the perfect moment to tell my story to a large group for the first time. *Lord, I will talk to Pastor Daniel about sharing my story on Sanctity of Life Day*, I prayed. I closed my Bible, feeling the weight lift from me now that I had a plan. I was thankful, though, that Sanctity of Life Day was in January, eight months away.

I put it out of my mind … until one day in the beginning of December I remembered the promise I'd made to God and Pastor Daniel. Dread filled me, but I knew to keep the story to myself—to hide my light—would be to disobey God.

On the day I was to speak, the reality of what I was about to do hit me. I was about to be incredibly vulnerable with our congregation, and my children did not know about my abortion. Even though they would be in children's church when I shared my story, I knew I had to tell them what I was about to reveal, so they could hear it from me in private and I could answer any questions they might have. I didn't want them hearing it from anyone else at church. At that time they were ten, seven, and five years old, old enough to understand what abortion was in age-appropriate ways. I feared they'd see me differently and be hurt and angry with me. After all, I had robbed them of another brother or sister.

On the way to church I cried as I explained what abortion was and about the terrible decision I'd made. I said I would never make that choice again, and I was looking forward to seeing their brother or sister in heaven someday. I told them I knew Jesus had forgiven me, and I asked for their forgiveness. My children were quiet for a while, trying to make sense of it, but when they climbed out of the car, each of them hugged me. "I'm sorry you had to go through that, Mommy," they said. "I love you. I forgive you."

With their forgiveness, I felt stronger as I walked into the sanctuary that morning. And as I told my story of looking for love in all the wrong places and getting pregnant at age fifteen, I only saw two emotions on the faces in the audience. The first was compassion. People saw me, knew my story, and hurt *for me*. I wasn't expecting that.

The second emotion was sorrow. The tearful faces of numerous women in the audience displayed the same heartache, shame, and regret I had experienced, and later after the service—and through the coming weeks—one by one these hurting women approached me. They told me their stories, which were similar to mine, and I was able to pray with them and share about the healing and hope found in Jesus. Some even signed up for a post-abortion Bible study.

Afterward I realized my greatest fear—people's revulsion—never materialized. In all the various reactions from those in church, there wasn't one negative comment. Many people said my story helped them recognize a second victim of abortion—the mothers. My story helped them understand that women who chose abortion often make that choice out of fear or shame and they suffer greatly.

As I've continued to tell my story, I've seen that mix of compassion and heartache on the faces in every crowd. And each time I speak at least one woman lingers and waits for the crowd to leave before approaching me. And as I hold her hands and look into her face, I'm able to tell her there's forgiveness and grace waiting for her too.

WHEN OUR PAIN MEETS ANOTHER'S

When I told my story at the luncheon Kelly attended, I could have shared only the high points. It might have been entertaining, but it never would have impacted Kelly's heart and encouraged her to reconsider having an abortion. Instead, I shared about the pain of my bad choices and took those in the audience back to a time in my life when I felt alone and afraid. So when I talked about my second teen pregnancy and how God gave me a beautiful son, the attendees knew about my mistakes and could share in my joy.

True connection happens when our pain meets another's. Jesus knows this. Many times in the Bible we see how sharing stories of healing can impact those around us.

One thing I love about Jesus is that He often approached people the world had written off—those whose sins made them untouchable. One of them was a demon-possessed man. Mark 5 tells the story.

Jesus was stepping out of a boat when a man filled with a legion of demons came to meet Him. The man lived in the tombs, and the Bible states that he was so strong not even chains could hold him.

Day and night he wandered among the tombs, crying out and cutting himself with stones.

> When he saw Jesus from a distance, he ran and fell on his knees in front of him. He shouted at the top of his voice, "What do you want with me, Jesus, Son of the Most High God? In God's name don't torture me!" For Jesus had said to him, "Come out of this man, you impure spirit!"
>
> Then Jesus asked him, "What is your name?"
>
> "My name is Legion," he replied, "for we are many." And he begged Jesus again and again not to send them out of the area.
>
> A large herd of pigs was feeding on the nearby hillside. The demons begged Jesus, "Send us among the pigs; allow us to go into them." He gave them permission, and the impure spirits came out and went into the pigs. The herd, about two thousand in number, rushed down the steep bank into the lake and were drowned. (vv. 6–13)

The men who were tending the pigs rushed off and reported what had happened, and many of the townspeople came to see. When they saw the man sitting and talking with Jesus and in his right mind they were afraid. How could this be? When they heard the story, they begged Jesus to leave. As He was leaving, the man—Jesus's newest convert—said he wanted to go with Him. But Jesus had a different plan.

> "Go home to your own people," He said, "and
> tell them how much the Lord has done for you,
> and what mercy He has shown you." So the man
> went away and began to proclaim throughout the
> Decapolis how much Jesus had done for him. And
> everyone was amazed. (vv. 19–20 BSB)

The story of the woman at the well is similar. Like the demon-possessed man, this woman was untouchable by society's standards. Not only had she been married five times, the man she currently was living with wasn't her husband. Everyone in town knew this. On top of that, this woman was a Samaritan. (In those times Jews were not supposed to associate with Samaritans.)

So when Jesus asked her for a drink, the woman, used to being an outcast, expressed her surprise. He responded, "If you only knew the gift God has for you and who you are speaking to, you would ask me, and I would give you living water" (John 4:10 NLT).

When the woman realized Jesus knew all about her, she called Him a prophet and accepted the living water He offered her.

What happens next tells us that this woman's encounter with Christ transformed her.

> Just then his disciples returned and were surprised
> to find him talking with a woman. But no one
> asked, "What do you want?" or "Why are you talk-
> ing with her?"
>
> Then, leaving her water jar, the woman went
> back to the town and said to the people, "Come,

see a man who told me everything I ever did. Could
this be the Messiah?" They came out of the town
and made their way toward him. (vv. 27–30)

These two stories bring me to tears. Both the demon-possessed
man and the woman at the well were feared and despised by their
communities. It couldn't have been easy for them. Returning to the
people who had mocked them, tormented them, and shunned them
couldn't have been easy, but they did it. Jesus so transformed them
they couldn't keep what He'd done for them to themselves.

I wonder, would we share our stories more if we truly understood how exceptional it is that God has transformed us? I fear we
often view sin on a sliding scale. In our minds a person who lies and
is prideful is less of a sinner than someone who murders, is filled with
demons, or is a habitual adulterer. Yet in God's eyes all sin is vile.

Isaiah 64:6 says, "We are all infected and impure with sin. When
we display our righteous deeds, they are nothing but filthy rags.
Like autumn leaves, we wither and fall, and our sins sweep us away
like the wind" (NLT). But when we come to Him, God replaces our
impurity with purity. He gives us a sound mind and clean heart. He
removes our darkness and fills us with light.

That light of Christ, though, is meant to be shared. Jesus doesn't
heal us just so we can feel better; He wants us to tell others what
He has done for us. He wants our vision to expand so we see those
around us who need to hear our stories. He wants to use those stories
to open doors that other hurting people can walk through to find
healing and hope for their own tormented hearts.

I don't know about you, but I used to wonder why God always seemed to use other people, but never me. Then I realized He was waiting for me to act on what He'd already told me to do to serve Him: be the light.

Ann Voskamp asked, "What if instead of waiting for good enough things to happen to us, we could be the good thing to happen to someone else who is waiting?"[1] Think about that for a moment. What good things might happen if you shared your story? You—your words—could be the good thing that happens to someone else today. My story was that "good thing" in Kelly's life.

I love *The Message* translation of 2 Corinthians 1:3–5:

> All praise to the God and Father of our Master, Jesus the Messiah! Father of all mercy! God of all healing counsel! He comes alongside us when we go through hard times, and before you know it, he brings us alongside someone else who is going through hard times so that we can be there for that person just as God was there for us. We have plenty of hard times that come from following the Messiah, but no more so than the good times of his healing comfort—we get a full measure of that too.

Just as you've received healing comfort from Christ, you can offer the same to others.

YOUR STORY, YOUR LIGHT

What has God done in your life? Where has He healed you, forgiven you, protected you? That is the story you need to share. Our stories assure others we've been where they've been, we understand. They also offer hope that healing and change is possible.

Maybe you feel like your story isn't "big" enough or miraculous enough to make a difference in other people's lives. You're willing to reach out to another person, but you question whether your story will have much impact. If that's you, I want to share some insight I gained at a writers' conference.

During a workshop, my friend Robin Jones Gunn pointed out that we all have events and "themes" in our lives others can connect with. What did she mean by "themes"? In literature a theme is the story's overriding lesson. While a plot is the action or events that happen, the theme is the message readers walk away with when the story is finished. It's a virtuous takeaway the character (if fiction) or author (if nonfiction) discovers, either in a spoken or unspoken way.

Robin asked each of us to create a simple time line of our lives, noting the highs and lows. Then we wrote down the themes each of these highs and lows uncovered for us. As I followed her instructions, I realized that Jesus had redeemed the low points in my life by using them to make a difference in the lives of others (my high points).

Here is a sample of what I wrote down that day:

Life-changing events: Teen pregnancy (low point) and mentoring teen moms (high point)

Themes: Knowing loneliness, longing, and embarrassment, and discovering that Jesus can fill our empty hearts

Life-changing events: Abortion (low point) and helping others with post-abortion healing (high point)

Themes: Making decisions in fear, living in regret, and then experiencing the hope and healing Jesus brings

Life-changing events: Not knowing my biological dad (low point) and then adding to our family through adoption (high point)

Themes: Feeling unwanted, then learning that God is our Father, and that He builds families

My teen pregnancy embarrassed me … until I started working at Hope Pregnancy Center and mentoring teen moms. My abortion only brought shame and pain … until I led post-abortion Bible studies. Not knowing my biological dad only brought feelings of being unwanted and unworthy … until I understood that God was my Father. All this transformation came from God. As I stepped out to follow God's Word and told others what God had done in my life, He used those low points to help me connect with others and make a difference in their lives, to bring light to others. "Preach from your weakness and you'll never run out of material!" says Robert Madu.[2]

Recently I asked my Facebook friends to share how God had transformed their lives and how hard events, mixed with God's healing, led to ways they could make a difference. Here is what a few of them said:

- "I attempted suicide at sixteen, and now I try to provide hope to those struggling with mental health issues today. After Robin Williams's suicide, my story was publicized locally to give others hope."

- "There was a time when I was nearly homeless, but by God's grace He set me and my little sons in the care of a loving family. I have a heart for the homeless and sometimes volunteer at our local women's shelter. God sets the lonely in families."

- "I am a warrior who's survived sexual, physical, and emotional abuse. I used to think I was alone during my horrific childhood and that God had forgotten me. In reality He protected me time and time again from death. I now show women there is hope in the future and for breaking the cycle of abuse and let them know they are never alone."

- "I'm an immigrant. I came to this country with a hope of a better future. I had to learn English, and I worked my way up from the bottom at my company into management. I now work closely and mentor others (especially immigrants) and help them build their future in this country and hopefully take away some of the prejudice and discrimination that so many face when they speak with an accent."

These are just a few of the dozens of stories people shared with me. And on my Facebook page, something beautiful happened. As people shared their stories, others commented. They reached out to each other. They compared stories, offering help and hope to each other. Heart connections were made. I was seeking a few quotes and ministry began to happen right before my eyes.

Another friend wrote me privately, and said, "Tricia, you asked about people's life themes, and I have only recently thought about this. I sometimes used to think that God couldn't use me the same way He could use someone who came from a troubled family or an abusive situation because they were the ones who truly had the testimony of God's amazing compassion and healing. But just recently I have begun to realize that *because* I didn't have those situations and came from a relatively secure, loving home, I am now able to be an anchor or rock to some of the hurting people in my life. I can be that stability they need when they don't have it."

I encourage you to do this assignment yourself. Your themes will reveal the stories you need to tell—stories others need to hear so they'll know not to give up and learn how to turn to Jesus for hope, healing, and answers.

Just as I had no idea how my words impacted Kelly, you may have no idea how your words can impact someone now or in the future. We just have to trust that at the right time God will use what we have to offer. As 2 Corinthians 9:10–11 says, "This most generous God who gives seed to the farmer that becomes bread for your meals is more than extravagant with you. He gives you something you can then give away, which grows into full-formed lives, robust in God, wealthy in every way, so that you can be generous in every way, producing with us great praise to God" (THE MESSAGE).

Lives change when we share life, light, and truth with each other. But the impact of sharing our stories doesn't stop there. When we tell others our stories, it reminds us of all the ways God has redeemed our low points and of what we learned about Him. Knowing your life themes fosters gratitude and thankfulness, and can provide a glimpse of how God might use you in the future.

You have a story to tell. The question is, are you willing to step out of your comfort zone and put aside your pride to share it?

Don't believe the lie that you have to be perfect or have to complete an evangelism course before you're able to share the good news of Jesus. I love what Matt Chandler said: "It's Jesus that saves, not my presentation of him."[3] And I'm thankful for that. For so many years I imagined that God uses important people to do big things for Him; then I looked in the mirror and realized it wasn't how important I was, but how willing I was.

Jesus comes alongside us in our pain, shame, and sin so we can do the same for others. God is the Father of all mercy, the God of healing counsel, but how are people going to know that unless we share our personal stories with them? How can those in our community see the difference—feel the difference—that Jesus can make in their lives unless we tell them? Today is a good day to start telling.

FOR REFLECTION

1. Think back to a time when someone's story encouraged or helped you. Why did their story impact you?

2. What holds you back from telling your own story?

3. Think back to a time when you dared to tell your story to another person. What happened? Is there anything you wish you would have done differently?

4. How has God been generous with you? What has He given to you that you can give away?

ACTION STEPS

1. Write a list of major highs and lows in your life. What themes do you see? How can your story make a difference in someone else's life?

2. Who in your life needs to hear your story? Prayerfully ask God to prepare you and give you an opportunity to share your story with that person.

3. Is there a part of your story you need to tell your family? Pray about how and when God wants you to share. Create a plan to make that happen.

6

All the World

I wasn't one of those kids who felt called to missionary work at a young age. In fact, whenever a missionary spoke at our church and asked who felt called to foreign missions, I'd often pray that I *wouldn't* feel God tap my shoulder. The missionary life didn't sound romantic or exciting. It sounded like a lot of work. I didn't like the idea of leaving a comfortable life for the unknown.

Even after I dedicated my life to Jesus, mission work wasn't on the agenda. I was perfectly happy to share Him with the kids at vacation Bible school and the young women who walked through the doors of Hope Pregnancy Center.

There was only one problem—Mark 16:15: "He said to them, 'Go into all the world and preach the gospel to all creation.'" *Sigh.* That's a pretty clear directive! But I appeased my conscience by telling myself the neighbor down the street was part of "all the world" too.

The first time I traveled internationally, I tagged along on a research trip with two writer friends. On the trip of a lifetime, we traveled through six European countries in seven days. Exploring famous sights and tasting new foods, without a care in the world, thrilled me. Then reality hit as we drove from the Czech Republic to Austria. On that dreary, rainy day in May, a young woman stood alongside the roadway, shivering under an umbrella.

My friend Anne explained, "She's a prostitute. Prostitution is legal in the Czech Republic, so Austrian men cross the border, hire a girl, and then take her into the woods." Then I noticed another young woman, and another. Reality shattered my heart, and I dropped my head in shame. I'd happily done all the touristy things without a thought for the hurting, needy people of this post-Communist country. I prayed for the young women as we passed. I wanted them to know God was *for* them. I wanted them to have hope and find freedom. But what could I do? I was just a young mom with little kids who'd head back to the United States the next day. As someone with a painful and broken past I wanted to rescue them, but how? I felt powerless to do so.

I returned home and life continued, but God kept bringing those young women, and the Czech Republic, to mind, prompting me to pray. I learned that after forty-one years of Communism in that country (from 1948–1989), Christianity had declined, and now fewer than 1 percent of all Czechs are Christians. At the time I had no idea what God had in store for me, my family, and that country. As always, God didn't disappoint.

GO!

God desires us to share the good news with the world. Jesus's parting words before He left earth weren't happy or encouraging, but a command: "Therefore, go and make disciples of all the nations, baptizing them in the name of the Father and the Son and the Holy Spirit" (Matt. 28:19 NLT). Yet how seriously do we take His words? Not seriously at all.

We often appease ourselves by praying for missionaries and giving to them financially. Yes, this is vital. But is it enough? Can we honestly read this scriptural directive and believe that we shouldn't—at the very least—entertain the idea that maybe God wants *many more of us* to *go* into the broader world? After all, we have something amazing to offer. First, God. Second, truth.

When we share the truth of God's Word with those who've never heard it, we're sharing a more joyful way of life. We offer what can't be bought: the keys to an eternity with Christ. People desperately need to hear our message, but we come up with all types of excuses not to go and tell them. And it's not as though we have to set off on a ship, like a hundred years ago, when missionaries packed their belongings in their coffin, because they knew they'd never see family or friends again. From most places in the world, we can maintain constant communication with our loved ones. Unless you are visiting the more tribal areas of Africa, Tibet, and Papua New Guinea, modern conveniences like electricity, running water, and the Internet are accessible. While it *is* emotionally and spiritually challenging, these days much of mission work is hardly "roughing it."

So why aren't we willing to build relationships and share the good news about Jesus in other parts of the world? Here are a few reasons I've heard:

- It doesn't fit with our agenda.
- It costs money, and it's a lot of work.
- We may make fools out of ourselves, find ourselves struggling with communication, or feel uncomfortable and out of place.

And all of these things are true for missionaries. But are those reasons really greater than God's call? Sometimes God even leads us to scary places and challenging situations because it's part of the whole adventure of following His greater call. It's thrilling to see God work in amazing ways, especially when we feel we are limited in what we have to offer. Often, these areas are exactly the best part of the journey, our most treasured parts, when we look back on them.

The last time I checked, I'm pretty sure God's Word didn't say, "Go and make disciples of all the nations if you have purchased everything you need and have some extra money. Or … if you have fulfilled all your goals and have some extra time. Or … if you totally grasp another culture so you're sure to fit in." I'm pretty sure His Word simply says, "Go."

Why else are we so reluctant to share God's truth with the broader world? Because we look at God's directives and consider what following them will *cost* us. Most of us think following this instruction is an option. But is it?

First Peter 2:9 says, "But you are a chosen people, a royal priesthood, a holy nation, God's special possession, *that you may declare the praises of him* who called you out of darkness into his wonderful light." Accepting Christ automatically signs us up to join His mission of reconciling the world to God. Jesus made this clear: "Jesus said to them again, "Peace be with you. As the Father has sent me, even so I am sending you" (John 20:21 ESV).

Most of us have memorized John 3:16, but how often do we take it to heart? "For God so loved *the world* that he gave his one and only Son, that whoever believes in him should not perish but have eternal life." The Bible is God's love letter to hurting hearts from all nations—a love letter we have the privilege to deliver. When we proclaim God's Word to those who need its message, we work alongside God Himself—something no other religion can promise.

When we step out in this way, it is less about what we give up (money, time, our own priorities), but more about what we gain: the ability to see Jesus at work in the world and the opportunity to participate in that work. We'll most likely face hardships, but we'll also experience the joy, love, and compassion of Christ in ways we never have before. As we obey Him in this area, God fills us up with more of Himself, so we have more of Him within us and more of Him to give others.

THE CALLING

So what did "being called to international missions" look like for me? It wasn't a grand or glorious moment. It happened, in fact, while I was sweeping. I'd been leading a study based on Henry Blackaby's *Experiencing God*, and something from the previous week's lesson wouldn't leave my mind: "When God honors your church by placing a new member in the body, ask God to show you what He is up to. He wants to touch your community and maybe even the world through your church."[1]

When Sona joined our church, I knew God was up to something. She was the only immigrant in our whole congregation and was from the one place I thought and prayed about often—the Czech Republic. (What were the odds?) So as I swept and cleaned up after Wednesday night supper, I couldn't shake this thought: *There's something to this. God is up to something.* I offered a quick prayer: *Lord, I know You brought Sona to our church for a reason. I also know You've given me a heart to share Your love with the Czech people for years. Please, Lord, show me what to do with this.*

Immediately a thought flashed into my mind: *Mission trip to the Czech Republic.* Possibly the fastest answer to prayer I ever received, I knew the thought was God's response because the idea of a mission trip (to anywhere!) had never entered my mind before that moment.

As I continued to sweep, I dared to believe that God had bonded my heart to the Czech Republic for a reason. It seemed He had been orchestrating events, and I was just one piece of a bigger plan. In a leap of faith I told God I was willing to serve Him in the Czech Republic. But when? How? I didn't know anyone from the Czech Republic, other than my church friend, let alone a missionary whom I could serve alongside.

I didn't have to worry, though, because God soon connected all the pieces.

I talked with my husband, Sona, our pastor, and the missions team and gained their support to explore what a mission trip would look like. Soon, I'd gathered others who wanted to go (including my kids, who were preteens and teens, and my husband). Next, a mutual friend connected us with a missionary family in the Czech Republic who needed people to lead an English camp. The team they'd counted on coming had backed out at the last minute. They'd felt certain they'd have to cancel the camp when they received our inquiry: "Do you need a missions team? We already have one forming."

So six months after the idea popped into my head, nineteen of us were sharing the good news of Jesus on the other side of the world. One day, we stood on the streets of a town called Hradec Králové and passed out Bibles written in both Czech and English. As I held a stack of Bibles in my arms, I called out to passersby, "Would you like a free Bible? Would you like a free Bible?" We also handed out information about free English classes and Bible lessons. As I stood there, I felt God's pleasure. God loves the Czech people and wants them to know His truth.

I'd said yes to God and became a short-term missionary, and the moment I sat face-to-face with a woman who had questions about God and the Bible, I knew I was in the right place at the right time. There was no other place I'd rather have been.

PART OF A CONTINUING STORY

One of my takeaways from the *Experiencing God* study was this exhortation: "When you see the Father accomplishing His purposes around you, that is your invitation to adjust your life to Him and join Him in that work."[2] I had never thought about that before, but recognized its truth. *God is always at work around us, accomplishing His great purposes.* We can have our own goals and fight to do our own things, or we can join Him in His work.

When we fight to do our own thing, it may or may not be the right thing. But when we join God in His work, it is always the right thing.

When we fight to do our own thing, it may or may not succeed. But when we join God in His work, it will always succeed.

When we fight to do our own thing, we're the main character in the story. But when we join God in His work, we're reminded that we're just supporting characters.

When we fight to do our own thing, our vision reaches only as far as we can see. But when we join God in His work, His vision is far-reaching, covering continents and generations.

This truth became real after I returned from the Czech Republic, only to discover that years before, God had also called my friend Robin to the same country. Every time I remember this story, I tear up, because it reminds me how God's plan expands over generations.

I've asked Robin to tell you the part she played in God's great plan.

> When I was a student attending a Bible college in Austria, an opportunity came up for me to transport Bibles behind what was then known as the Iron Curtain. Czechoslovakia was then under Soviet rule and Bibles were scarce. Four college-aged women made up our team, and we would

take turns driving a large camper filled with hidden Bibles to a small town to the east, near the Polish border. My heart leaped at the chance to smuggle thousands of Bibles into the country and secretly deliver them to a pastor.

However, when the mission organization in Germany trained us for the journey, I realized that if we were caught, we'd spend two years in prison. If we compromised the safety of the pastor or the believers in the underground church, their punishment would be much worse.

I don't think I've ever prayed as much as I did during the eight days it took us to get through the border and drive to our designated town. Not one of us had all the information about where we were going and who we were meeting. One of us knew the name of the pastor, one knew the name of the town, one knew the time and location where we were to meet, and one of us knew the code phrase we were to use on the telegram back to Germany once we were safely inside the country. All went as planned.

However, the first few days of our trip we were followed, presumably by a KGB agent. But once we left Prague and headed north, the round-faced man in the small black sedan stopped tailing us. We stopped at a cemetery outside our destination, removed the Bibles from their hiding places, and stuffed them into large garbage bags. That night, at 11 o'clock, we drove through town slowly and stopped at a corner in a residential area. A short man stepped from behind a big tree, and we opened the cab door. He slid in and stayed low on the floorboards. In whispered German he told us where to go. We drove for many miles, out into the countryside. His directions led us to an apple orchard shrouded in an autumn fog. Two men waited for us beside their car.

The delivery of the Bibles was swift. We handed the eight bags out the side door of the camper; the men stuffed them into every opening of their compact vehicle. Not a word was spoken. Then the three men came to us, stepped up into the camper, and embraced us. I felt the tears of one of the men as they fell on my neck and slid down my back. They drove off, and the four of us spent the night in our camper in the orchard. I remember crying under the blanket and not being able to sleep. What if we were caught? Worse, what if those men were caught? I remembered how Peter, in the book of Acts had said, "We must obey God rather than men" and that was why he kept preaching after the authorities had told him to stop.

The thing that was most unsettling to me was the fact that at home, in my comfortable southern California bedroom, I had a half a dozen Bibles on my shelf. How often did I read from any of them?

In this part of the world, these Christians were willing to risk their freedom and even their lives just to have a copy of God's Word.

Several days later, while trying to exit the country, we were detained and questioned at the border. Nearly all our money was taken from us, but none of us cared. We returned to the mission in Germany with changed hearts. I have never forgotten what a treasure the Bible is. It is alive. It is active. It has great power. I have never again taken for granted what a solemn, entrusted privilege it is for us to have the Bible in our own language.

In the wonderful way God works, He sent me and my team to the very town Robin had smuggled Bibles into—Hradec Králové! How do I know this? As Robin said, only one person on her team knew where they were going. Guess who that was—Robin! (Don't you find that amazing? I do!)

She had to smuggle Bibles into the city through the darkness. But only a couple of decades later, in that same town, my teammates and I were able to stand on the street and hand out Bibles in the light—with the government's permission!

God's goal has always been the same—for His children to carry His Word, His truth, around the world. What might have happened if I had not heeded God's call? What might have happened if Robin hadn't?

Robin's story deeply moves me because it reveals how God was already at work in the Czech Republic generations before I ever stepped into the scene—and His work there continues still. What an *honor* to be a part of this story. I was just a young mom who told God, "If you can make anything with my life please do," and He was gracious enough to answer me in this amazing way. It makes me wonder what He would do with more of us—if we just paid attention to the stirrings in our hearts and dared to take leaps of faith.

CHOSEN FOR HIS PURPOSES

My daughter Leslie had just turned sixteen years old when we first went to the Czech Republic, but for years before that God had been telling my heart that He planned to use her in a big way.

One day, when I was busy at my "work," Leslie asked for help with her homework. The interruption frustrated me at first, but then a still, small voice filled my mind: *What if your greatest work has nothing to do with you … but with her?* I felt the Holy Spirit saying, "What if all the work you're doing is just a foundation for *her* great work?"

I understood what the Spirit meant. I tended to view my greatest ministry work as that outside my home, but maybe the most important thing I was doing for God's kingdom was simply loving the kids in my own house. God had powerful things He wanted to do in and through my children, things I couldn't imagine when they were small.

At the time I had no idea how God planned to use Leslie. When I look at her life now, it's clear I was just a building block God used in His greater plan for the Czech Republic—a plan she is invited into, as well. My faithful steps led to her faithful steps. God has duplicated my mission-heart within her—and expanded it. But instead of telling you her story myself, I'm going to let my daughter tell you.

I was twenty years old when God asked me to move to the Czech Republic for a year as a short-term missionary. One of the passages He used to move my heart was Romans 10:9–15:

> If you declare with your mouth, "Jesus is Lord," and believe in your heart that God raised him from the dead, you will be saved. For it is with your heart that you believe and are justified, and it is with your mouth that you profess your faith and are saved. As Scripture says, "Anyone who believes in him will never be put to shame." For there is no difference between Jew and Gentile—the same Lord is Lord of all and richly blesses all who call on him, for, "Everyone who calls on the name of the Lord will be saved."
>
> How, then, can they call on the one they have not believed in? *And how can they believe in the one of whom they have not heard? And how can they hear without someone preaching to them?* And how can anyone preach unless they are sent? As it is written: "How beautiful are the feet of those who bring good news!"

A perfectionist, I like to have every detail planned out, and yet that was impossible in this situation. I was in my last year of college, working part-time, taking a course on world missions, volunteering with my church's youth and dance worship groups, preparing to move, and trying to figure out how and when I could do the fund-raising I needed to do.

One day I heard God say, "Trust Me. I will provide all you need. I promise." And so I didn't plan any fund-raisers. I'd written a blog post about my decision and told my church about it, but I did nothing else to raise my support. I left that in God's hands, and I prayed.

As the months slowly ticked by, money trickled in. Just four weeks before my departure date, I had about 20 percent of my support raised. As I prayed about my need, God asked me, "Leslie, if you don't have all the money in your account, will you trust Me to provide? Will you go, knowing that you only have the first couple of months covered, and rely completely on Me?"

I took my fear and laid it at His feet. "Yes. I'll still go. I trust that You'll take care of me."

A week later the woman assisting me with the visa process emailed me. She wanted me to send her copies of my bank statement to show that I had at least 80 percent of the money I needed for the year in my account.

My heart sank. I had no idea that this was a requirement, and I didn't have the money. I had only a few hundred dollars in my account, with a bit more pledged. Where would I get the thousands of dollars required? *God, I know You promised You will provide. Please show me how this should happen.*

After the prayer, I felt a shift in my heart. Though the situation hadn't changed, my spirit was at peace, knowing that God would follow through on His promise.

About ten minutes later, I was reading through my email again and felt nudged to check my spam box. I opened it, and inside was a notification from PayPal: a donation that covered *all* the money I needed had come through the link I'd posted on my blog (which by the way didn't reveal the amount of money I needed). Everything, all at once! And the most incredible part? It had come through about half an hour before I even knew I needed it.

A friend I hadn't seen in more than five years made the donation. When I contacted him and asked what inspired him to send it, he said, "I just want you to know you were big a part of God's plan in my life to know Christ as my Savior. And I hope you will let God use you so lots of others will know Christ."

I met this friend, Semi, one summer when we were both working at a Wendy's fast-food restaurant. Wendy's had a summer work-exchange program, where young adults from other countries could come to the United States and work for two months. Since I was a trainer, I often trained these people, one of whom was Semi. One day as I was showing him how to make a burger, he noticed the cross necklace I was wearing, and in his broken English he asked, "Why would you wear a cross like that? Isn't it just another tool to kill someone, and isn't it like wearing a gun pendant around your neck?" Since he didn't speak English that well, I pulled down one of the burger-wrapping papers and, using the mustard bottle, drew a picture to explain the gospel and why the cross symbolizes hope through Christ's death.

Semi visited church with my family a few times and had several conversations with my dad about what it means to believe in Jesus. Later that summer, he returned to his home in Azerbaijan. He later became a Christian and occasionally followed my blog. When he saw my post about leaving for a short-term mission trip, he was reminded of how God had used me in his life, and he wanted to support me in telling more people about Jesus Christ.

Later I asked him how he finally came to know God. He said, "When I came back to Azerbaijan, I got into depression, and everything was terrible. Sometime in December I took the Bible in hand once again, after maybe five years from the last time. [We had given him a copy before he went back home.] I prayed and was so attached to the Bible, and I started to see what God was actually doing after that. I started to see Him in my life. Knowing how life is short, and everything will pass, I want to devote my life to Him as my Savior and spread the news about Him. Missions is something in my thoughts."

WHAT GOD DOES

Sometimes God asks us to go around the world to share the gospel. Sometimes He sends the world to us. Sometimes He asks us to go down the street. And sometimes He wants our steps to set the foundation for someone coming behind us, following our footsteps, and then venturing out on her own. Someone with beautiful feet, bringing the good news of Christ with every step she takes.

I'm not sure about you, but tears fill my eyes as I read Leslie's and Semi's stories. One thing Leslie didn't mention is that Semi grew up in a Muslim community, and when he came into our home he related to Islam. How beautiful that the gospel can be shared through an eloquent sermon in a cathedral or a hamburger wrapper and a mustard bottle in a fast-food restaurant. I love how God used a new believer to help a young woman move across the world to spread the gospel!

After finishing her year in the Czech Republic, Leslie returned home, but she soon felt God lead her to return there as a career missionary. She's lived there four years now and serves in the local church and volunteers in numerous ministries. She's also recently become a professor at a university. Yes, my young daughter now serves other young people in an official capacity, and the friendships she builds are opening doors and fostering relationships. Not only that, but Leslie met and married a wonderful Christian Czech man. She's committed to spending her life there, spreading the love and light of Jesus.

Every time my daughter leads someone to Christ, walks someone through baptism, or shares the good news of Jesus with someone who's never heard it before, I feel as if it's part of my story too. Leslie's story grew out of mine, and when Semi dared to listen to God's voice and sent that donation to Leslie, he joined the story too. It's as if my tears softened the soil and she's plowed it, making it her life's work. And I can't wait to discover what God does in and through my other children's lives, things I see Him already starting.

God invites anyone with a listening heart to join His ongoing story. I know this to be true.

God moved my heart and caused me to fall in love with the people of the Czech Republic, knowing that my daughter would someday live there.

God stirred me to lead a mission trip to the Czech Republic, knowing that on that trip Leslie would glimpse what serving in that country full time would be like.

What I saw in part, God saw in whole. If I hadn't taken that first step, I never would have known what God would do. I would have missed the adventure, and Leslie might have missed all God has led her into since then.

So, dear friend, pay attention when God breaks your heart. He's inviting you to join Him in prayer and action. Be aware of the people He brings into your life. If you meet an immigrant, ask God how *you* fit into His work in that person's life and country. Cling to the messages God whispers to your soul, and don't give up even when the work gets hard. Sometimes walking it out means taking leaps of faith, but God will always catch you. And remember that your life is not solely about you. You are part of a continuing story God has been scripting for generations.

FOR REFLECTION

1. Is there a part of the world that really connects with your heart like the Czech Republic connected with mine? Why do you think God has given you this bond?

2. If money and time were no issue, would you go on a short-term mission trip? If so, where would you go and what would you want to accomplish?

3. What Scripture verse about missions most pricks your heart?

4. Do you know a missionary you can support? What could this support look like?

ACTION STEPS

1. Is there a person from another country in your church or neighborhood? Pray and ask God how He may use you and your church to impact that person and his or her native country.

2. Research a short-term mission trip to a place God has put on your heart. What would it cost for you to go on that mission trip? What would it require? Prayerfully ask God to show you how to best serve unbelievers around the world.

7

Wrestling to Give

I am exuberantly happy when I watch my family gathered around the table enjoying a meal. I love to see my children dressed in clean and comfortable clothes. Even as a teen mom I found great purpose in pulling my newborn son's clothes out of the dryer and folding them. Caring for another person felt good. Most of us do long to help others, but knowing how to do it can be daunting on many levels.

Even today one of my greatest joys is meeting the needs of others. So a few years ago when I traveled with a group of bloggers through the Kibera slums in Africa, I felt a deep helplessness. The needs were so many, so great, I couldn't begin to meet them. *Dear Jesus*, I asked, *what can be done here?*

I pray that same prayer every week when I head into inner-city Little Rock to meet with the young moms in our support group. I've seen where young women turn when they feel they have no one who will help.

"This lady contacted me on Facebook. She saw I was a single mom and told me she knew a way I could make money fast," one young mom confessed. "She introduced me to some people, and I sold my body. It was just horrible. I can't believe I did that. And now this lady won't leave me alone …"

People in need are easy prey for those who want to exploit them for their own gain. When men and women reach the end of their resources, any promise of a way out of hunger and/or homelessness looks like a lifeline. Many reach out to anyone throwing them a rope, not realizing it's a chain that will entangle them, pulling them even further into dark depths.

Most teen moms in our support group come from single parent homes or live with an extended family member. They face continual loss because of addictions, violence, and abandonment. Caught in a generational cycle of poverty, they have no idea how to escape. I want to help them, but I also worry about causing more harm than good.

THE STRUGGLE

If I give them too much, will they stop trying to be resourceful? Will they look to me to save them instead of to God? I don't want these young women to become dependent on the gifts of strangers or the system; I want them to learn to be independent and to provide for their families themselves.

Yet I sometimes wonder if such concerns are just an excuse for not helping more. After all, showing compassion to the poor is part of our job description as believers.

Then the King will say to those on his right, "Come, you who are blessed by my Father; take your inheritance, the kingdom prepared for you since the creation of the world. For I was hungry and you gave me something to eat, I was thirsty and you gave me something to drink, I was a stranger and you invited me in, I needed clothes and you clothed me, I was sick and you looked after me, I was in prison and you came to visit me."

Then the righteous will answer him, "Lord, when did we see you hungry and feed you, or thirsty and give you something to drink? When did we see you a stranger and invite you in, or needing clothes and clothe you? When did we see you sick or in prison and go to visit you?"

The King will reply, "Truly I tell you, whatever you did for one of the least of these brothers and sisters of mine, you did for me." (Matt. 25:34–40)

If Jesus walked through my front door, I'd have no problem giving Him everything I have to give. So why do I struggle to give to others? I confess that sometimes I look at the needy and am tempted to think, *They just need to stop their destructive behaviors and get their act together.*

I don't know about you, but for me some of the hardest Scriptures to come to terms with are ones that address helping the poor.

Maybe because I know the cost of "my" gifts. To give something someone *needs*, I may have to give up something I *want*. If I buy someone's meal, I'll have less money for those jeans I've been eyeing or that new novel that's coming out. Sad, but true.

Maybe because I've traveled to a dozen countries around the world, including Kenya, South Africa, Jamaica, Belize, Mexico, and Honduras, I'm aware that the impoverished in the United States are actually doing pretty well compared to the rest of the world. Even though this country is far from perfect, we have governmental agencies that watch out for disadvantaged families, we provide free education, and we have countless churches and community organizations that strive to care for people's basic needs. But I forget the system is sometimes broken. I also forget God asked *us* not *the system* to care.

Or maybe this particular mandate seems harder for me than others because I have a lot of material things, and I like my belongings. I have more than enough clothes, and I live in a six-bedroom, three-bathroom home. We're not all sharing a two-room structure cobbled of scrap lumber and tin. Even with eleven people, our family still has space to spread out. When I visited schools in Kenya, I noticed I had more books and homeschool materials for my seven kids than one school had for seven hundred students.

Whatever the reason, I struggle to know how to care for the children God has entrusted to John and me while also giving to people living in poverty.

I think God understands this struggle, and that's one reason why this directive is so clear.

> But if anyone has the world's goods and sees his
> brother in need, yet closes his heart against him,

how does God's love abide in him? Little children,
let us not love in word or talk but in deed and in
truth. (1 John 3:17–18 ESV)

Could this verse be any more direct? Here the God of love urges His followers—His children—to be people of love. And to be people of *action*. Those verses are convicting, but I find the verse that comes right before it to be more so: "This is how we know what love is: Jesus Christ laid down his life for us. And we ought to lay down our lives for our brothers and sisters" (v. 16).

Most of us will not be called to literally die for a friend, family member, or neighbor. (Aren't we glad about that!) In comparison what God asks us to do seems far less costly: *simply share what we have.* Jesus laid down His life for us; can't we head to the store and buy fifty dollars of groceries for someone in need?

LIVING ON LESS

I used to think I understood what it means to be poor. When I was growing up, my mom and stepdad struggled to make ends meet. The first childhood home I remember was the single-wide mobile home our family lived in. Each year when school started I received one new outfit; all the rest of my clothes came from yard sales. When I was in the sixth grade, my stepdad was without work for a time and our family lived on government assistance, which meant we received government surplus food. Have you heard about the food assistance of the early 1980s? Big blocks of government cheese and white-labeled cans of food.

But I didn't truly understand generational poverty until a few years ago when our family moved to Little Rock and became part of Mosaic Church, a multiethnic and multi-economic congregation. Some of our members were affluent; many more had very little. A few church members were even homeless, living in vacant lots near the church.

Five months after we started attending Mosaic, I launched Teen MOPS, a support group for teen mothers. Most of these young ladies lived below the poverty line. Many lived with their children in places that lacked running water or heat. Most depended on others for transportation and food. Some wore ill-fitting clothes and transported their kids in carriers (not car seats) that looked to be thirty years old.

After our meetings I'd lie awake at night and pray for these families. I wanted to walk out God's directive to share with those in need, but I didn't know what that should look like. I longed to help them, but I didn't want to make it all about me, about making myself feel better just because I did something. I wanted to assist with immediate needs, but I also wanted to help these young women rise above their situations. I wanted to tell them that even though they'd had kids at a young age, their lives didn't have to be over. They didn't have to accept that they'd live in poverty and work minimum wage jobs for the rest of their lives.

Lord, what can I do?

IT DOESN'T TAKE MUCH

One day a young mom, her head hung low and shoulders slumped, started attending our support group. We were eating a meal, and she made herself a plate. But instead of sitting down to eat, she covered that plate with a napkin, set it aside, and fixed a second plate. I guessed then that she didn't have enough food at home—if any. The set-aside meal was for the next day. I ignored the extra plate as I sat down to talk to her. I learned she was a single mom to two little girls. They were staying in the local Salvation Army shelter, but she was hoping they could get their own place soon.

When she finished eating, I led her to a back room. It was once a Sunday school supply closet, but we'd turned it into a store for the moms.

"All the clothes and items here are free," I said. "Just let me know what you need and what sizes. I can help you find some things. We also have diapers we'll give you at the end of the night."

She looked around, eyes wide. "All of this is free?"

We picked out a few things together, and her steps weren't so labored as we went into the classroom for the night's meeting.

Everything I'd offered this young mom—the clothes, the meal, the diapers—had been donated by people in the church and community to help teen moms just like her. Because of caring people, she had found a little help.

That night, I slept a little better. I couldn't do everything for everybody in need. After all, many in Little Rock had needs just as great. But I had done what I could. A young woman had stood before me, and I had offered her what I had: the material goods God provided as I followed His mandates.

One of the most important lessons I've learned as I've sought to walk out God's directive to give is that the act of helping is a balancing act.

A BALANCING ACT

The first year I headed a Teen MOPS group the other volunteers and I ran ourselves ragged. Most of us had never worked with the disadvantaged before, but we'd joined together to do what we could. We gave young moms rides to appointments, picked them up for our meetings, and bought groceries. I pushed my own kids' needs to the side—after all, wasn't helping a young mom whose electricity had been shut off more important than spending one-on-one time with one of my kids?

I believed I had to do something for everyone who had a need. Yet many times, instead of feeling I was making a difference in these women's lives, I felt used. For example, one day a young mom called and said she'd just been discharged from the hospital with her newborn baby and she didn't have any food. I loaded up my kids, drove to the store, spent over a hundred dollars on food, and took it over to her.

She was living with her boyfriend at his mother's house. I loved on the baby for a minute and then unloaded the food from my car. Ten seconds after I placed the food on the counter, no less than six adults emerged from various parts of the house and started pulling things from the bags. Suddenly reality hit. The food I'd purchased would be gone that day, and very little of it would nourish the young mom. Despite my good intentions, I hadn't really helped her. I had taken money out of my food budget to care for someone else, and she'd still wake up hungry tomorrow.

When the other support group leaders and I compared notes, I discovered I wasn't the only one running around attempting to meet all the needs. Some volunteers quit, and sometimes I wanted to quit too. There were just too many needs and only one me.

Have you ever felt that way when you look around? Sometimes we witness desperate circumstances face-to-face. Other times we see them on our Facebook feed or on the nightly news. The struggles of the world can overwhelm us, yet each of us only has so much to give.

Walking away from these young women would have been easy, but I knew that wasn't the answer. What was the answer? I took that concern before God and prayed.

Over the next few days He showed me that I'd been trying to do too much. My calling wasn't to make life easier for every teen mom in Little Rock. Instead, He'd called me to start and colead the teen mom support group meetings. I had taken it upon myself to do more, but God had originally called me to address their emotional, relational and spiritual needs, not just their physical ones.

I had tried to meet all the material needs of these young moms, but they were poor in other ways as well. Poor in their relationships with God. Poor in their relationships with themselves. Poor in their relationships with others. Poor in answers and hope. God is a relational being, and we are created in His image. All of us—the poor and disadvantaged included—were made for relationships, and relationships offer the most life-changing way to help other people.

God reminded me that our support group's primary goal was to point these young moms to Jesus, the One who would never leave them or forsake them, the One who'd be there for them, even when we were no longer in the picture. This was the number one way we could ease these young women's burdens.

The next important thing we could do was help these moms build relationships with others. Through our weekly meetings they drew closer to each other and to the older women who ran the support group. As those of us who led the meetings shared about our own weaknesses and struggles, these teen moms realized that we didn't have our act together either and we needed God and each other just as much as they did. Within these relationships the young women learned more about themselves, discovered their worth, and found dignity that could empower them to make good choices to alleviate their own poverty.

"Until we embrace our mutual brokenness, our work with low-income people is likely to do more harm than good," wrote Steve Corbett in his book *When Helping Hurts: How to Alleviate Poverty without Hurting the Poor … and Yourself.* "I sometimes unintentionally reduce poor people to objects that I use to fulfill my own need to accomplish something. I am not okay, and you are not okay. But Jesus can fix us both."[1]

Teen MOPS had to return to God's original vision for us—educate, inform, and inspire. We committed to doing what we could: educate young moms on everything from disciplining children to writing a resume, inform them of community resources, and inspire them to know God and to be who God created them to be. Knowing we can't meet all their needs, we are doing what God has called us to do and trusting *Him* to do the rest.

When I look back on all I did outside of our meetings to try to help young moms, I realize my actions stemmed from a mix of pride, a mini god-complex (*I can be the answer to their need!*), and a battle with my own insecurities and inadequacies. I also had a sincere desire to help, but just did not understand how. I wanted the young moms to trust and like me so they'd keep attending the meetings.

Consider your own motivations. Why do you want to help the poor? Do you think you know what is best for others? Do you desire to feel as though you're achieving something important? Are you trying to pursue a noble cause? If we reach out for any other reason than love and a heart for service, we are doing it wrong.

The next fall, when a new year of meetings started and our focus returned to the core of our mission—it worked. We watched as teen moms became better parents. They connected with community resources to meet their physical needs, and they formed relationships with the leaders and each other. Most rewarding of all, many of these young moms grew in their relationship with God.

This gives me great joy. Five years later we are still serving mothers.

WAYS TO MAKE A DIFFERENCE

God may not ask you to start a teen mom support group, but you can still show love and care for the poor. Whether in a group or one-on-one, the best way to help someone is to connect with them. Here are some ways to do that.

1. SEEK TO UNDERSTAND BEFORE YOU JUDGE

It's easy to make judgments that the poor around us are irresponsible and unwilling to change. Some will make bad choices, even sinful ones. But as you seek to understand individuals and their hearts, you might discover what each person needs most is hope that things can be different.

How would you feel if your mom just lost her job, your sister needed school supplies, your two kids needed clothes and food, and you didn't have the resources to help them … yet someone offered you a wad of cash for an hour with your body? I'm not excusing sin—people still have a choice—but I'm starting to grasp why people sometimes make sinful choices. This strengthens my dedication to offering help so the young women I know won't have to turn to desperate means.

While our support group has helped many teen moms, the leaders have also benefited because their involvement has fostered a better understanding of the complexities of poverty. Many people believe that those in poverty simply need to decide to do better. We forget that poverty itself may make people more likely to make bad choices out of desperation. And what we may not realize is poverty also taxes the brain.

I recently read this online in *The Atlantic*: "Researchers publishing some groundbreaking findings … have concluded that poverty imposes such a massive cognitive load on the poor that they have little bandwidth left over to do many of the things that might lift them out of poverty—like go to night school, or search for a new job, or even remember to pay bills on time."[2]

The poor often carry such heavy burdens they may not even hope there's a better way. They feel nothing will ever change. At Teen MOPS we educate young moms in ways that alleviate their poverty, and they listen—and keep coming back—because of relationship.

2. ASK BEFORE YOU ASSUME

Our own observations may mislead us. People in desperate circumstances may seem standoffish, causing us to think they don't want a relationship. In reality, they may feel embarrassed about their situation or worried that if we truly knew them we'd judge them more. Seek to be a friend, and ask if they are open to that.

3. SET BOUNDARIES, REALIZING YOU CAN'T HELP EVERYONE

Over and over again people came to Jesus because they wanted something from Him. Crowds followed Him, not always to hear His messages, but to see the miracles. It isn't every day you see the blind receive sight or the lame dancing a happy jig.

People in need surrounded Jesus, but He often zeroed-in on just one person. He even sought time alone, especially so He could hear from His Father. If anyone literally could help everyone, it was Jesus, but He set boundaries and chose to connect one-on-one.

4. BELIEVE GOD CAN PROVIDE

Not too long ago, I learned about a young mom of two, one a new-born, who had no heat in her home. I woke up one night worrying about her, but within a few minutes felt the urge to pray instead of worry. I turned her need over to God, confident He loved her and cared for her even more than I did.

Two days later a friend called. "I have a woman who wants to help young moms beyond diapers and clothes," she began. "Do you know of any needs?" Did I ever. I spoke to the woman my friend mentioned and explained the needs of this mom who had been on my heart. Within days the gas bill was paid, the house was warm, and other needed resources were given—with promises for additional help.

God cares about people in need, and He loves listening to our prayers! He can provide more than we think or imagine. He also wants to get others involved in this work. When we trust God, He proves Himself faithful. And when we tell others where these good gifts came from, He gets the glory, not us.

5. KNOW THAT SOMETIMES YOU ARE THE ANSWER TO PRAYER

There are times we only need to pray, and there are times we need to be the answer beyond prayer. If I feel God nudging me to offer a young mom help outside of our meetings, I do. Setting boundaries is important, but it's also okay to step outside those boundaries when you sense the Holy Spirit tug on your heart.

MODELING HOW TO GIVE

It's been important for everyone in our family to find ways to give to the poor, because that is what God asks us to do. It's also vital we parents model giving for our kids so they grow into adults who not only read God's Word but also walk it out.

One way we can help our kids understand God's care and compassion for the poor is to let them see God's Word working in and through us. That's why I often pray for opportunities to involve my kids in giving to those in need. And sometimes the best opportunities come when I least expect it.

One day I attended Bible study with my three youngest, who were in preschool and kindergarten. We had to leave early for a doctor's appointment and were going to miss the meal the Bible study members regularly shared together. But, knowing we were leaving early, the leader had packed lunches for us. (We live in the South, after all. True Southern hospitality!) On the way to the appointment I stopped by a Mexican bakery to pick up pastries to take home for Grandma. They are her favorite.

The doctor's appointment didn't take long, and after I buckled my kids into my minivan I turned to see a man in a wheelchair patiently waiting next to the driver's door. He was an older African American, possibly a veteran, as he was missing one of his legs.

"Ma'am," he asked politely. "Would you happen to have any food in the car?"

My face brightened. "Yes, yes I do!"

I reached into the bag with our food, pulled out one of the sack lunches, and handed it to him. He peeked in the paper bag and his face brightened. Then I opened the pastry box and pulled out the largest donut. Chocolate frosting drizzled down the top. I handed it to him.

"Ma'am." Tears rimmed his eyes as he gazed at the donut. "Is this cream-filled?"

"Yes, sir. I believe it is."

Then, with a bright smile that filled his face, he took a large bite. "Thank you, ma'am. Thank you."

He backed up his wheelchair, and I got into the car. I spied him smiling and eating that donut, and my heart was full. And as I backed up I heard a voice from the back seat. "Mama, who was that man?"

And that's when I realized my kids had witnessed the entire interaction.

"Well, he probably lives around here and doesn't have money for food. Isn't it amazing that God had provided food for us to give him?" I said.

The other kids chimed in:

"Mama, let's take him home!"

"Mama, he can sleep under my bunk bed!"

"Mama, can we take him dinner tonight?"

I explained the man couldn't come live with us, but maybe we could think about ways to help other people like him. Over the next few weeks we packed bags of items we could keep in our car. The bags contained water bottles, wet wipes, granola bars, toothpaste, toothbrushes, soap, and a few other items. We then looked for people to share them with.

Since then, I've discovered several of my friends are teaching their children similar lessons. I was talking with my friend Jamerril about how she opens her kids' eyes to the needs around them. She told me:

> We are always on the lookout for single moms who need firewood to heat their homes and jackets for their kids. (The Lord usually sends us some.) We also try to meet the need for food in a practical way by purchasing large totes and filling them with nonperishable food items. It may not be ultra-healthy or perfect, but I know moms who would love to have a big case of macaroni, Ramen noodles, and oatmeal cream pies to shove in the back of the pantry for the hard seasons.
>
> Also, if we see people holding up signs for food or money, we usually stop and give them food. Sometimes it might be a couple pounds of bananas. One time we handed out a bunch of apple pies from McDonald's.
>
> At times we've seen a mom and a child hauling in lots of clothing to the laundromat. I'll give one of the kiddos cash to put in the mom's windshield wiper to bless her when she and her kids come out. We try to just do it in and about living daily life when possible.

Jamerril's example is just one of many. KerryAnn, who is often homebound, knits with her kids so they can provide hats and scarves for those in need. Ashley created Spend, Save, and Give banks for her kids and taught her daughter to use the Give money to sponsor a child in need. Lisa and her kids serve at the local food bank, and they often step forward to pay for groceries when they see the person's money is short.

While each family has chosen a different way to care for those in need, the important thing is that we're modeling for our children what giving looks like. When we teach our children to give as they are able now, it'll train them and show them how to love and care for the poor now and in the future.

AN IMPORTANT TRUTH

As I seek to give to those in need, God keeps reminding me of an important truth: *No one can do everything, but everyone can do something*. When we're caring for the needs of the people God brings into our path, we can trust He will provide the wisdom and strength we need to do so. It won't always be easy, but with God's help it will be doable.

What is God calling you to do? How is He asking you to help and love the poor? Seek Jesus and pray He will give you His heart and show you what He wants you to do. When you walk out God's mandate to care for the poor, your heart becomes more like Jesus's. And lives will be changed—especially yours.

REFLECTION QUESTIONS

1. What do you find challenging about giving to others?

2. Think about a time someone gave to you in order to alleviate a need you had. What difference did it make in your life?

3. Why do you think God asks us to give to others when He is capable of taking care of people's needs without our help?

4. When it comes to giving, how can you set up boundaries while also being generous?

ACTION STEPS

1. Pray and ask God to open your eyes to the needs of an impoverished person today. Seek to build a relationship with that person.

2. Talk to your kids about giving to others. What are their ideas for giving to someone in need?

3. Memorize 1 John 3:17–18: "But if anyone has the world's goods and sees his brother in need, yet closes his heart against him, how does God's love abide in him? Little children, let us not love in word or talk but in deed and in truth" (ESV).

8

Welcoming the Vulnerable Ones

Tears filled my eyes and my body trembled as I sank to the floor. I felt drained, depleted. I collapsed in the middle of the hardest year of my life. I cried out to God over and over again to keep me together enough to just make it through the day.

We had welcomed four girls from foster care, aged ten to fifteen, into our home through adoption, and I'd never felt so assaulted in my life. After suffering abuse and neglect during their early years, our new daughters had been rescued by social services only to face more trauma. Shuffled between foster homes, shelters, and residential treatment homes, they experienced abandonment over and over again by well-meaning adults who promised to adopt them and keep them safe, only to disappoint them. During their many moves the girls' possessions were often lost, broken, or stolen. When we adopted them, the girls were living in a children's home, separated into different cottages by ages.

It's often said that hurting people hurt people, and I know that to be true. I dealt with our adopted daughters' harsh words, accusations, and unacceptable conduct on a daily basis. One of them so feared opening her heart to yet another mother figure—only to be crushed—that she continually pushed me away. I poured out love, only to be met with hostility. I offered compassion and tenderness, only to be ignored—not looked at, not talked to, not acknowledged for days at a time. Some of her sisters joined in her harsh response. I hadn't done anything to upset them, but they acted as though I had. Why? Because they only knew two things: (1) they had to stick together, and (2) mothers couldn't be trusted.

I felt defeated; my heart was broken. At times I wondered if John and I had done the right thing.

OUR DECISION TO ADOPT

Many people grow up knowing they'll adopt someday. That wasn't me, and that wasn't John. After all, our household was full: the two of us, our three kids, and my grandmother.

As I've mentioned, my grandparents were an important part of my life. My mom and I lived with them during my first years. My grandparents' home had always been a safe place for me growing up, and their daily habit of Bible reading and prayer provided a great example for me. Caring for my grandmother after my grandfather died was an opportunity to give back to someone who had done so much for me. More than that, Scripture says when we care for the widow, it pleases God. "If a widow has family members to take care of her, let them learn that religion begins at their own doorstep and that they should pay back with gratitude some of what they have received. This pleases God immensely" (1 Tim. 5:4 THE MESSAGE).

So adoption had never entered my mind. But then one day, God spoke to me as I read an article in *Woman's Day* magazine about the number of abandoned baby girls in orphanages in China. Lacking love, attention, and physical contact, many of these babies died. Suddenly I looked at all I had—a nice, warm house, plenty of food, two vehicles, happy kids—and it seemed selfish not to open our home to adoption. Surely we had enough room in our lives and heart for one more.

A verse I'd memorized resonated in my mind: "If anyone, then, knows the good they ought to do and doesn't do it, it is sin for them" (James 4:17). Once God pricked my heart and nudged my conscience concerning the needs of the vulnerable, I couldn't stop thinking about all the children who need a safe and loving home. God's heart for the vulnerable confronted me in Scriptures like these:

> Pure and genuine religion in the sight of God the Father means caring for orphans and widows in their distress and refusing to let the world corrupt you. (James 1:27 NLT)

> Learn to do good. Seek justice. Help the oppressed. Defend the cause of orphans. Fight for the rights of widows. (Isa. 1:17 NLT)

Give justice to the poor and the orphan; uphold
the rights of the oppressed and the destitute.
(Ps. 82:3 NLT)

Widows and widowers. Orphans. The disabled. Refugees. The
chronically or terminally ill. The poor and destitute. People with
great needs surround us. Some, like my grandmother, are within our
own families.

As I read God's Word, I didn't read: "If your personal dreams
are fulfilled and you're financially stable, then consider opening your
home to an orphan." No, God's directives aren't suggestions. It's not
acceptable to stay silent, to do nothing in the face of evil and injustice, to not open our homes to the vulnerable. He wants us to act.

I had to do something. The problem was, John didn't share
my conviction that we needed to adopt a child. He loved God passionately and cared about orphans, but John's plan was to become
personally involved after retirement. He wanted to retire, move to a
Third World country, and open an orphanage. More and more, to
me, that plan seemed distant and unreachable.

I brought up the idea of adopting once or twice over the next
five years, but John still didn't feel the time was right. Instead of
nagging or trying to talk my husband into it, I prayed. I wanted
John to be drawn to adoption because God had stirred his heart,
not because I had nagged him. Every time I had pushed to get my
way in my marriage, it had not turned out well. Adoption would be
hard, and would require both of us being committed. John had to
be all-in on this decision. When problems happened I didn't want
him to blame me.

Then one day, out of the blue (or so it seemed), he asked me, "Are you still open to adoption?" It took me about two seconds to answer *yes*.

I had to ask, "Why now? What changed?"

A friend who had recently stood by his dying father's bedside had told John about the experience. The dying man had planned to retire and dedicate himself to full-time service. "Promise me," the father told his son, "that you won't wait until retirement to follow God's calling on your life."

"I know the time to follow God's call is now," John said, "not waiting for a mythical time in the future that may never come."

Before we proceeded with adoption, we talked it over with our children, who were teens and preteens at the time, explaining what we felt God was calling our family to do and why. All three were open and excited to the possibility of gaining a brother or sister.

It seemed nothing was holding us back, and I pictured a new addition to our family within the coming year. But it didn't happen like that.

A STRETCH OF FAITH

I wrongly assumed that since God had called our family to adoption, everything would fall into place. But the process took far longer than we thought, and it stretched our faith. We would wait another three years before we opened our home to the child our hearts longed for.

John and I hired an agency to move forward with a Chinese adoption. Yet right when our paperwork was finished, China stopped placing matches for healthy baby girls. I was crushed. I'd waited all that time. We'd spent all that money, and now the adoption wasn't going to happen. The day I learned we wouldn't be adopting from China anytime soon, if ever, I crawled under my comforter and bawled my eyes out. I didn't understand why this door would close. Weren't we trying to live out what Scripture had instructed us to do?

It made no sense. Did God give me this desire only to slam the door in my face? I thought about families I knew whose adoptions had gone seamlessly. *Why them and not us, God?* I felt abandoned and rejected.

Finally, after crying and complaining for what seemed like hours, I surrendered. *Lord, I feel You've called us to adopt, but I turn it over into Your hands. I trust You will give us the child You have planned for us.*

Jesus's sweet presence touched my heart and eased my soul. Even though I had my time frame, I had to trust that God had His. We weren't going to miss out on the child God had for us just because things weren't moving as quickly as I desired. I imagined God holding our future child in His hands until the time was right.

My heart lifted. As hard as it was, I trusted God and His ways. This wasn't something I could accomplish with my own effort. I had to turn it over to God.

Hours after I relinquished my desires to God, a friend called. She knew a birth mom who planned to place her child for adoption and was seeking a family. Would we be interested in meeting the birth mom? I was almost afraid to hope.

John and I met with Jenna many times, and after a few weeks she chose us to adopt her baby. Almost three months after I surrendered our future child into God's hands, I held a brand-new baby girl in my arms. Alyssa is a pure joy and a gift. She is the child God had planned for us, and it wasn't by the means I had planned. Now I can't imagine life without our girl.

A few years later we adopted through foster care a sibling pair, a two-year-old and a five-year-old. And most recently we adopted the sibling group of older girls, also from foster care. Our one yes turned into many yeses. We'd opened our hearts to the vulnerable ones, and now we have a full, overflowing house.

HELP FOR THE VULNERABLE ONES

Why does God so frequently in His Word direct His followers to care for orphans and widows, the disabled and destitute? Because they, of all those on the earth, are most vulnerable. We must step forward to care for them when they cannot care for themselves.

My heart aches when I think about the vulnerability of so many, especially orphans. One night during the first two weeks after we brought her home, five-year-old Bella confessed, "It's scary having to go to a new place." After reading through her files I knew she'd had to fall asleep in twelve different beds, in twelve difference places, all in twelve months. As I tucked her in, I tried to imagine how she must have felt, having no assurance that she was truly safe.

Elderly men and women can face similar fears. Some aren't even able to perform simple, daily functions without help. After a lifetime spent caring for others, they now must be cared for, and their only hope is that someone will be tender and gentle with them. No wonder God asks us to care for the vulnerable, to be His hands and feet, sharing love with those He desperately loves.

My eighty-seven-year-old grandmother can no longer do things like clip her own toenails or wash her own laundry. How humbling it must be to have to ask for help with such things. And that's why I don't wait for her to ask; instead I attempt to anticipate her needs and offer help.

I do the same with my children. I imagine myself in their place and try to understand how everyday issues in normal family life can be overwhelming for those who haven't experienced it. I attempt to offer compassion and love. I try not to focus on problems my child is causing, but instead imagine a young adult, years from now, who feels settled and loved and can face the world with basic skills and the knowledge that he or she will always have a mom and a dad to run home to.

When I look around my home today, I see eight people—my grandmother and seven children—who have a different life from they otherwise would have because of the choices John and I made—choices that led us on a radical adventure as we opened our home.

As John and I walk out God's good plan for us, we've experienced Him in ways we wouldn't have if we focused only on ourselves, on making our lives comfortable and self-fulfilling. I've never needed God so greatly as I do when I walk out this mandate. I've never depended on Him more. I've cried to Him in desperation; I've turned to Him in prayer more than ever. And I'm not the only one who has discovered God in the midst of great challenges.

My friend Kathy wrote:

> God's divine plan for me, as my husband is bed-bound in hospice care, is to meet his needs and allow his

last days to be spent at home. I have known that my personal ministry has always been to my husband—and caring for him now is truly a divine extension of that call and assignment from God. I treasure the opportunity to serve the Lord this way. He is pleased when we take care of those He loves who cannot care for themselves … the elderly, the disabled, the ill … anyone in need. I've learned that when performing the most difficult types of care, when I put on praise music, God's presence transforms the unpleasant and difficult care into an offering of worship for His honor. I know my husband's care will become more demanding and my ability to provide for his needs must come from the Lord, our Provider and very present Help at all times.

God faithfully meets us when we care for the vulnerable. When we are close to the brokenhearted we find Jesus there. As Psalm 34:18 says, "The LORD is close to the brokenhearted and saves those who are crushed in spirit." Most of us tend to draw away from uncomfortable things, but when we dare draw close and help a vulnerable person, we discover God's sweet Spirit there, strengthening us and bringing peace in the midst of hardship.

WILL I BE ABLE TO DO THIS?

Perhaps you've considered adoption or caring for a sick or elderly relative, but what that would require overwhelms you. You've weighed your options, and your worries and fears make commitment hard. I understand.

Deciding to bring my grandmother into our home brought considerations of time and space. For a season she shared a room with our preteen daughter, which meant my daughter mostly slept on the couch because Grandma snored so loud. Caring for my grandmother's daily needs was easier in the early years, but it has gotten tougher as she's grown older. When she first moved in, she was only seventy years old. She still liked to cook and fold the laundry. She was in relatively good health. But she's now seventeen years older, and needs a lot more help from me on a daily basis. Because she's diabetic, I monitor her medications and food. Tracking her medication is easy, but keeping an eye on her food intake is a constant challenge as she likes to sneak snacks into her room.

As she's aged, Grandma has regressed, and sometimes I feel as though I'm dealing with another kid. I have to remind her over and over again to take a bath, and that she can't eat all the cookies in the pantry. But these issues are minor compared to the challenges others face when caring for their parents.

My friend Tammy told me, "It is frustrating when you are the only sibling doing all the caretaking. It is hard to keep positive. My sister has not lifted a finger to help. It's also intense blending different generations. Sometimes my mom treats me like I'm still a teenager, which drives my husband nuts. I work full-time, but Mom just wants me home sitting with her all the time. That's hard to do with a career."

"It was hard seeing my strong, independent father be ashamed to need help with personal care," adds another friend, Bonnie. "I did my best to guard his dignity at all times. I also tried to reassure him that I was privileged to provide just a fraction of the love and care he once provided me."

When you open your home to an elderly relative, you may have to give up a lot: space, time, and freedom. I can't just come and go as I please. If Grandma gets sick, I have to rearrange my day to take her to the doctor. She fell recently, and I had to manage her in-home therapy appointments five days a week. The work will only increase as her mobility decreases and she needs more hands-on care. But the uptick in care for my grandmother has been gradual, and so it has felt less challenging than the level of care our adopted children require.

When you adopt a child, you make a lifelong commitment that affects your present and your future. There is no walking away. To welcome a child into your family is to accept that child's needs, flaws, and dysfunctions. It's to carry that child's burdens as your own, not only for the next few hours or days but for the rest of your life. It's promising to offer a piece of your heart for forever, no matter how often it's trampled on.

Adoption often brings immediate financial burdens and emotional upheavals. Many adopted kids have special needs due to harm they experienced in the womb or during their early years. And no matter what you've heard, kids need more—much more—than love alone.

Lisa, an adoptive mom, recently told me, "Unconditional love will always be a blessing, but go into adoption knowing the saying 'all a child needs is love' isn't always true. You can love a child with all of your being, but he or she may need more. A child may need you to drive him to therapy because your love just isn't enough. Your child may bring emotional weight with her that she will carry for a lifetime, and you will be there to help teach her how to carry it and where to seek wholeness (from God). But you will have to let go of the dreams that you will rescue your child."

NEVER ALONE

Thankfully, God promises to guide us and help us as we walk out this directive. I turned to Scriptures like the following when the adoption journey became hard:

> And if you spend yourselves in behalf of the hungry and satisfy the needs of the oppressed, then your light will rise in the darkness, and your night will become like the noonday. The Lord will guide you always; he will satisfy your needs in a sun-scorched land and will strengthen your frame.
>
> You will be like a well-watered garden, like a spring whose waters never fail. Your people will rebuild the ancient ruins and will raise up the age-old foundations; you will be called Repairer of Broken Walls, Restorer of Streets with Dwellings. (Isa. 58:10–12)

While the above passage promises that when we spend ourselves on behalf of the vulnerable, we will be like a "well-watered garden," we fear otherwise. In *Sharing God's Heart for the Poor*

Amy L. Sherman wrote: "Our fear, however, is that in pouring ourselves out we will become empty and dry. We hold back from spending our lives on the poor, from pouring out that which is inside of us for fear that we won't have anything left. We worry that if we pour it all out, we ourselves will be dry."[1]

Sherman went on to tell the story of the widow of Zarephath in 1 Kings 17. A drought had devastated the land and God sent Elijah to her to ask for food and water. When he arrived, she told him, "As surely as the LORD your God lives … I don't have any bread—only a handful of flour in a jar and a little olive oil in a jug. I am gathering a few sticks to take home and make a meal for myself and my son, that we may eat it—and die" (v. 12).

Instead of seeking food from someplace else, Elijah promised that if she followed God's directive, the flour and the oil she had would not be used up, that they would be miraculously replenished until the drought ended. The woman had faith and fed the prophet and her family, not only that day but all through the drought.

Do you see the parallel between the challenge this woman faced in deciding whether to share her food with Elijah and the challenge we face in taking someone into our homes? We see the little we have to offer and the great cost of caring for the vulnerable, and the math doesn't work.

I too had many fears. What if my grandmother had a medical issue and I didn't know what to do? What if her forgetfulness created an unsafe environment for my family? What if I reached a place where I couldn't do it anymore?

What if our adopted children verbally or physically assaulted our other children? What if they couldn't progress beyond their past trauma and that negatively impacted our home environment? What if the stress of caring for them divided John and me? I feared our adopted children wouldn't bond with us and might seek out unhealthy relationships. I feared we'd be wrongly accused of mistreatment or our loving actions would be pushed away. I feared we'd do all we could, give all we could, love all we could, and it wouldn't be enough.

Yet John and I had to trust that God could take what little we had and multiply it. What we had in our own stores wasn't enough, but with God it became everything we needed.

What the widow had to offer wasn't used up because God Himself replenished what she poured out. And what John and I offer hasn't run out yet—and it never will—because when we reach the end of our resources of peace, love, patience, and strength, God will always show up. "This is the wonderful paradox of the Christian life. When we pour ourselves out, we do not become empty; instead, we become full," Amy Sherman also observed.[2]

Some days I don't feel I can handle my grandmother's needs, but as I step forward and serve her, I find I'm able to complete my tasks with joy. I'm reminded of all the care she's given me and thankfulness overwhelms me.

On days when I struggle emotionally I turn to Jesus, and He shows up there too, brightening our overcast home like the noonday sun. On days when my soul feels like a sun-scorched land, I go Jesus, whose living water never fails.

When I pour out love, honor, and tenderness on our kids, the Lord Jesus refills me with His Word and His Spirit replenishes me with His presence. Every day, it seems, I offer all I have, and the next day I wake up to discover I have enough resources and energy to carry me through.

MY HEART NEEDED HEALING TOO

As I answered God's call to care for the vulnerable, I discovered that despite all the spiritual growth and healing I'd experienced, I *still* longed for comfort, ease, and control more than I wanted to admit. I thought I'd learned to not worry about people's opinions—until four added children made it hard to walk through the house without stepping on dirty clothes, shoes, school books, and toys. I'd freeze every time someone knocked on the door, not wanting anyone to see the mess and judge how my house looked.

I thought I'd adjusted to stepping out of my comfort zone—until I attended therapy sessions with my daughters and listened as they battled with the impact of pain and abuse from their past. I felt completely lost, not knowing how to help.

I thought I'd adjusted to things being outside my control—until I did all the right things according to the parenting books (even the parenting books I'd written), and instead of accepting my care my daughters withdrew.

I thought I'd given up my desire for ease—until my grandmother needed my help for the twentieth time in a day, and I longed to just put my feet up and escape into a good book.

More than anything, I longed for comfort, ease, and control to return to my world. I wanted to be appreciated and valued and to feel a sense of pride that I could make everything better by doing the right things and saying the right things.

My heart needed a tune-up. Although the situation was hard on everyone else too, in my heart it became all about me. And God has used these challenging, outward experiences to calibrate my heart.

As Watchman Nee said:

> In order to serve God the inward man must be able to launch out. The basic difficulty lies in how the inward Man can thrust through the outward man. The former has been imprisoned for quite a long time and unless it can be released, there is no effective work which can be done. The bondage of the inward man creates a serious problem. In fact, nothing interferes with the work of God more than this. The outward man must be broken so that God may be manifested, the inward man may come forth, and God's work may be done.[3]

Mind you, anyone viewing my life from the outside would conclude that I was doing all the right things, yet despite God's work in my heart in this area, part of it *still* wanted to do more, to look better, and to gain attention.

First John 2:16 says, "For the world offers only a craving for physical pleasure, a craving for everything we see, and pride in our achievements and possessions. These are not from the Father, but are from this world" (NLT). Even as a Christian writer and speaker I gave the world what I knew it needed—Jesus—while I made myself as comfortable and well-liked as possible. I wanted to share Jesus with others, and I worked hard to do it, but I kept enough of a buffer around me that all the really difficult stuff stayed beyond arm's reach.

But one day as I peered into the defiant, hate-filled eyes of my teen girl, I realized I was not Tricia Goyer the author, Tricia Goyer the speaker, or Tricia Goyer the award winner and applause receiver. I was a hurting mom who didn't know how to help my hurting kid, standing in a house that no longer felt like my own because mess and clutter overwhelmed it. This new me had no time to step onto the stage to speak to crowds. I was just trying to make it to bedtime when I could slip away to dreamland and give my bruised heart a chance to heal from the emotional punches. But as we read in 2 Corinthians 4:8–12:

> We are hard pressed on every side, but not crushed; perplexed, but not in despair; persecuted, but not abandoned; struck down, but not destroyed. We always carry around in our body the death of Jesus, so that the life of Jesus may also be revealed in our body. For we who are alive are always being given over to death for Jesus' sake, so that his life may also be revealed in our mortal body. So then, death is at work in us, but life is at work in you.

John and I had followed the decree to care for the widows and the orphans because God said it and it was the right thing to do. We had no concept of all the unexpected God-gifts we would unwrap as a result. Yes, at times we were crushed, but we also have seen Jesus revealed in ways we'd never before experienced. I'm closer to God because of my pain, and I feel more alive than I ever have before.

When I opened our home to my grandmother, and then to our adopted children, I thought I was doing something for God—but really He was doing something for me. He was healing my selfish heart and teaching me that sometimes the hardest steps of obedience reap the greatest rewards. And sometimes the people who are the most challenging to manage end up being the ones who wrap around our hearts and never let go.

God is growing us to be more like Him. He is showing us His heart. He is molding us into His Father-image.

You should see the looks John and I get when people hear my grandmother has lived in our home for over seventeen years. The looks of disbelief transform into utter shock when they also learn we've adopted seven kids, most of them from foster care.

"Are you crazy?" people ask. And the looks in their eyes speak even louder: "You are fools."

Yes, we're foolish enough to believe we can make a difference in the world. We're foolish enough to believe God can do what the world says cannot be done, as we pile nearly a dozen broken, hurting people into one home and expect to not only survive but thrive. We're foolish enough to believe our pursuit of justice and kindness for those who didn't do anything to deserve their fate will reflect God's love in ways nothing else can.

God wants us to care for the widow, and for this season John and I know the most loving place for my grandmother is with us. Caring for her isn't just about making sure my grandma is fed, takes her meds, and stays safe. It's about showing Christ's love by putting her needs before our own. It's displaying a message that says all life is sacred, even life that is no longer productive by society's definition.

God also longs to put children into families, and through adoption He's expanded John's and my vision as parents beyond what we could have ever imagined. He's stretched our hearts more than we believed possible and enabled us to teach our kids what God's love looks like now and what His love provides for us for eternity. Adoption isn't just about giving children a home. It's about bringing them in and living a life that allows them to see God in us. It's granting them a chance to hear about God, trust Him, and accept His salvation, making their eternity secure. These kids have experienced the hard stuff of life, and we can point them to the good stuff, the eternal stuff.

The culmination of our partnership with God's work in our children's lives will come the moment they stand before God, and—if they've accepted Christ—He says, "Well done my good and faithful servant, enter into your eternal kingdom" (see Matt. 25:21). Our children will then walk into their true home—one that will be theirs for eternity.

And when it comes to my grandmother, I see these last years with her as ones where we are able to honor her when she feels useless and value her when she has seemingly little to give. Wouldn't we all like to be treated in such a way?

WHY WAIT?

There are children all around the world who need family, a home, and parents. In addition there are the elderly, disabled, and victims of abuse. Many searching souls have asked, "If there is a God, why do so many people suffer?" Yet this suffering is not part of God's plan. He's asked us, His followers, to do something about it. And we're the ones failing at our job.

I will admit that the lack of Christians obeying God's directive in this area angers me. I don't understand how we can see the injustice, oppression, and exploitation of those who are most vulnerable and simply look away. Why are the beds of retirement homes, orphanages, and children's homes filled when many Christian families have an empty bed in their home—or room to add one? *Justice, freedom,* and *peace* are easy words to declare, but when we ignore living them out we bind our very souls as we chain ourselves to comfort, self-indulgence, and ease.

What's God's request? "Defend their cause." For some families this means adoption or opening their home to another vulnerable person. For others it may mean supporting those who do. How can you start supporting them?

1. Make a meal.
2. Deliver a few bags of groceries.
3. Offer to take the kids on fun outings.
4. Babysit so the caregivers can have a break.
5. Give them gift certificates to local attractions.
6. Send notes of encouragement.
7. Show up to help clean or do a few loads of laundry.
8. Pray.
9. Ask them, "What more can I do?"

One of the sweetest things a family from church did was hand me an envelope filled with pizza gift cards. The note said, "When you need a break and have all those mouths to feed." Be creative with what you offer and give. We have no excuse for not doing something to help someone.

Rise up for the orphan's cause. Care for the elderly. Fight injustice. Do good. Don't look away. Don't hide in your comfort zone. Don't wait to follow God's call. Even though it may be hard, friend, don't miss out on the riches God has in store for you as you meet the needs of others.

"Blessed is the one who perseveres under trial because," we read in James 1:12, "having stood the test, that person will receive the crown of life that the Lord has promised to those who love him."

As you consider how to follow God's directives in your life, I'll cover you with this Franciscan prayer:

> May God bless you with discomfort
> At easy answers, half-truths, and superficial
>   relationships
> So that you may live deep within your heart.
>
> May God bless you with anger
> At injustice, oppression, and exploitation of people,
> So that you may work for justice, freedom, and peace.
>
> May God bless you with tears
> To shed for those who suffer pain, rejection, hunger,
>   and war

So that you may reach out your hand to comfort
them and
To turn their pain into joy.

And may God bless you with foolishness
To believe that you can make a difference in the
world,
So that you can do what others claim cannot be
done,
To bring justice and kindness to all our children
and the poor. Amen.[4]

FOR REFLECTION

1. Who are some of the vulnerable people in your life? Imagine yourself in their shoes. What are their worries? Their fears?

2. What are some of your greatest fears concerning opening your home to a vulnerable person?

3. When was a time you grew closer to God even in the midst of great challenges?

4. In what ways do we grow closer to God when we care for those who cannot care for themselves?

ACTION STEPS

1. Consider how God specifically has called you to care for the vulnerable. Do you feel called to open your home to the orphan or widow? What would that look like? If not, what could you do instead?

2. Make a list of ways you can help caregivers. Choose one way to help this week.

3. Offer your friendship to a caregiver, to an elderly person, or to an adopted child. Provide a listening ear and a safe place to connect.

9

Family Matters

As I write this book I'm under a deadline, which is nothing new. When I complete one writing project, it's time to start another, which is both a wonderful and hard place.

Here's a rundown of my typical day:

- writing in the early morning hours before the rest of the family is up
- homeschooling
- driving kids to therapy or wherever else they may need to go
- housecleaning, laundry, and cooking
- helping my grandma and spending time with her
- talking with or playing games with our older kids who are eager to connect when the little ones are finally in bed

- spending the last hour of my day with my husband as we talk, plan, and connect

One evening, in the middle of the fun and conversation, I wondered aloud about how much more writing I would accomplish if I wasn't playing board games with my older kids every night.

"Mom," my son Nathan responded, "at the end of your life you're not going to be thankful you spent more time at your computer. You're going to be thankful you spent time with your kids."

I raised a smart boy. He's right. Now that some of my children are adults, I better understand how quickly time passes. If I don't grasp these moments with my kids while they're still under my care, they'll slip through my fingers.

One of God's directives we often don't hear much about, especially in Christian ministry circles, is 1 Timothy 5:8: "Anyone who does not provide for their relatives, and especially for their own household, has denied the faith and is worse than an unbeliever." In this passage Paul generally spoke about caring for family members financially, but the concept applies to other types of care too: being present, listening, attempting to understand, and not being distracted by so many things.

When I was a young mom, I found it hard to be present to my kids—to play with them, listen to them, and just be with them. I am a woman of action—I like to get things done. For instance, I love having a clean house, and so I found vacuuming easier than sitting down to play a game with my kids. I love checking work projects off my list, and so I found working at my computer easier than snuggling with my kids on the couch to hear about their day. I love getting comments from readers, telling me how much my words helped, so I found giving advice on my blog easier than talking to my son about his struggles.

My heart aches now for all the times my mind wandered to a different place when my children wanted to talk. And even now, though my heart has awakened to the need to be "with them," when I am with them, I can still be tempted to think about other things. Added to my inclination to work rather than play are the distractions of cell phones and social media. Twenty years ago only my own ideas and plans distracted me; now I must add my Facebook friends and blog followers, many of whom have interesting things to say.

It's makes me wonder, *Is it possible to read God's Word, do what it says, and still make sure my family knows they matter? Is it possible to love and care for the world and, at the same time, make sure my heart and mind are fully present in my home?*

Can you relate? Have you fallen into bed only to realize you'd placed the most important people in your life at the end of the line for receiving your time and attention? God loves for us to embrace our callings, to work toward God-given dreams, and to love others who need us, but not to the detriment of those within our own home.

If we know what our friend on the other side of the country ate for dinner, but are unaware of our child's struggle with a friend at school, then we have a problem. If we know more about our girl-friends' troubles than we know about our husband's work challenges, then we have a problem. If we are quick to meet with a fellow church member who needs prayer, but are too busy to stop and pray with our kids before they take a test at school, then we have a problem. If we know more about the hardships of the characters on our favorite Netflix show than the needs of our parents or grandparents, then we have a problem.

Because I know myself, I pray this simple prayer every day: *Lord, bring my heart home.* In this, I ask God to show me when I have disconnected from my family and ask Him to help me reconnect with my loved ones, those living inside and outside my home.

I need Jesus's help to remember that despite all the good things I may be doing, if I am not tending to the most important relationships He has given me, then I am not doing as He asks. I'm also missing so much: moments and relationships I'll never get back.

BEING AN INFLUENCE

Our kids need our time, attention, and presence. It's critical we're fully present when we are with them. Being present means making eye contact with them instead of staring at our phones, greeting our children when they come home from school, telling them how much you love them just out of the blue. When we are connected with our kids, we have a better chance to influence their lives. When we give them rules, they resist less because they trust our hearts.

Think about it. You may have some influence on others in your work and community, but you'll never have any greater influence than in your role as a parent. There are other ministry leaders, writers, and Bible study teachers, but I am my children's only mother. And you are yours. Your influence with your children transforms their lives. Abraham Lincoln is credited with saying, "All that I am, or hope to be, I owe to my angel mother."[1]

Equally important is that we give our kids a foundation on God's Word and an example of walking it out. Our children's spiritual discipleship is our responsibility, not something we leave to a Sunday school teacher or Awana leader. After all, "Jesus said, 'Let the little children come to me, and do not hinder them, for the kingdom of heaven belongs to such as these'" (Matt. 19:14).

Our kids will be the parents, ministry leaders, missionaries, and work force of tomorrow. And no matter what they accomplish or don't accomplish, their life's journey will come down to one moment, when some day—at the end of their lives—they stand before Jesus and He says, "Well done, good and faithful servant." No college attendance, grades, job, or life calling compares with that.

Recently, a friend asked my daughter Leslie why ministry and service mean so much to her. "It's something my parents modeled and what we've always done," she answered. "From the books we read, the ministries we volunteered in, and the friendships we've fostered, I've seen it modeled." And that is what our kids need most: to see us walking out the Word of God and daring to do what it says. When this is important to us, it becomes important to them. The saying, "Do what I say and not what I do" never works. Instead, we should be able to tell our kids, "Do what I say *and* what I do." "Follow my example, as I follow the example of Christ," Paul told those he was leading in 1 Corinthians 11:1, and we should be able to say the same.

When I prayed for God to bring my heart home, it was because I was realizing that I needed to pay more attention to my children. I had no inkling the answer to that prayer might involve bringing my heart home to John as well.

HOME TO MY HUSBAND

For years I didn't realize that for me to fully love my husband and my heart to come completely home, God needed to clean out all the baggage I carried deep inside. For John to truly matter, I had to make room in my *whole* heart so I could give 100 percent to my marriage.

Even as I said my vows, I worried that our marriage might not last. I'd watched my mom and stepdad struggle for many years. They divorced just as John and I were starting our life together. In fact my stepdad told John *on our wedding day* that he was filing divorce papers. He waited to tell us until after the wedding, and wanted us to know he wouldn't be living with my mom when we returned from our honeymoon. How's that for horrible timing, right as I'm driving off to my happily-ever-after?

I tell people now that John had no idea what an emotional mess I was when we got married. I came with baggage, a whole dump truck full. No father nurtured me in my childhood. I became sexually active as a young teen, and I had more than one sexual partner during high school.

To say I had a lot of trust issues is an understatement. A wall as wide and tall as the Great Wall of China guarded my heart. When we married I'd been following and serving God for less than a year. Yet God gave me a man who was dedicated to me and who worked to draw me close.

A lot of joy came to our marriage once I found healing from the pain and shame of my abortion. Once those walls tumbled down other barricades fell with them. And while John and I enjoyed a good marriage, I had no idea my heart still needed a lot of healing; it had to do with all those bits and pieces of myself I gave away in my search for love.

One day in my Bible reading I came across Psalm 139:23–24, and I whispered it as a prayer: "Search me, God, and know my heart; test me and know my anxious thoughts. See if there is any offensive way in me, and lead me in the way everlasting."

I had thought my life was going well. I had a good marriage, good kids, a good church, a good teen mom support group, and a good writing and speaking ministry. I had no clue what God was about to uncover. In my opinion there wasn't much to search for. (What a joke!)

The very next day, a message from an old boyfriend popped up in my email. This was before Facebook, but he tracked me down through Classmates.com. He'd seen my photo and told me how beautiful I was. He claimed he had never forgotten about me. He said he believed we were always meant to be together. He was divorced, and he stated he named his daughter after me. (I'm not making this stuff up.)

Even though I should have deleted that email, I didn't. I emailed him back. I was flattered. More than that, seeing his name and reading those words released a flood of emotion. I felt like that fourteen-year-old girl again who just shared her whole heart and her whole body with someone for the first time.

Not only did we start emailing each other, we talked on the phone a few times. Although I told him I was happily married and loved my life, my heart pounded at the sound of his voice. He said he wanted to see me. I refused, but my resolve was weak. I knew I needed help, BIG help, and so I confessed to a few close prayer partners and then to John.

I'll never forget the pain on John's face when I told him all that had happened in the previous days.

"Do you still care for him?" John asked with tears in his eyes.

"I don't know," I managed to say. "In a way, yes, and I hate that I do."

John held me then and cried as he prayed for me. I hated myself for all the emotions churning inside. I knew the pain I had caused him. I promised to break off contact, and I did, but I still struggled. Part of me still felt like that teen girl inside who thought she'd found love. I'd still think of my old boyfriend, and then I'd pray about it and push those thoughts away.

I admitted this to some of my closest friends during our yearly prayer retreat. "After almost a year I still struggle with feelings for my old boyfriend," I confessed.

"That is unacceptable," one of them said, and then all the women surrounded me to pray. They prayed the bonds that held me to that man would break. They prayed I would give my whole and complete heart to my husband, once and for all.

That night I lay on an air mattress, thinking and praying, and I realized that part of me didn't want to turn over all my thoughts and emotions to Jesus. I wanted to cling to the romance of a "first love." Even though our relationship had been unhealthy, at the time I felt more loved and accepted than I ever had before. Years later, I felt flattered he still thought of me and "loved" me after so much time.

And so, I asked Jesus to show me how He saw that relationship. Then in my mind I saw His heart breaking. I realized Jesus had been with me during those years when I searched for love. Jesus had wanted me to turn to Him, to find love in Him, and instead I'd turned to a teen boy.

I imagined Him weeping as the relationship became physical, knowing all the heartache and pain it would bring. I imagined Jesus wishing I would let Him give me the tender care I longed for. And as I took in Jesus's truth, I realized that past relationship was not a sweet, fairy-tale romance. Far from it. It was an inappropriate relationship. It was an older teen taking advantage of a younger teen barely into high school. It was sin.

I asked Jesus to forgive me for trying to find love in all the wrong places. I thanked Him for not giving up on me and for wooing me until I accepted His love. I also thanked Him for my faithful husband, and I prayed Jesus would dig out any old connective roots from old relationships so I could turn my heart completely over to John.

When I woke up the next day I felt different. I felt free. In order to tend to my husband and kids first, I had to give up what had held back my heart. I went home from that retreat as a new wife, with a full and complete heart to give to my husband.

Not only that, I began to trust John completely. I used to worry that if I did the wrong thing or said the wrong thing, John would abandon me, just like every other man in my life. Seeing John's love, even in the midst of my hurtful actions, allowed me to trust him more. I can now be myself, share my feelings, and turn to him in my hurts without fear he'll walk away. Our relationship deepened, and our dependence on each other grew.

I truly believe God waited to lead John and me to adoption until our marriage was strong enough to handle it. We needed each other's complete trust. This adoption journey would have crushed me if I hadn't had John to walk through it with me. We crash into bed at night and pour out everything we've seen and experienced during the day. We talk through ideas and plans for how to handle our new normal, and we pray together. We *have* to depend on each other—we have to stand as a united front before these emotionally traumatized kids.

As He had so many other times in my life, God waited to bring the next big thing until He knew my mind, heart, and spirit were ready for it. God didn't use me to write and speak until I healed from my abortion. He didn't call me to help start a crisis pregnancy center until I walked through my grandfather's death and realized how our actions greatly influence other people's eternities. He didn't open doors for me in the publishing world until my heart dove deep into other people's stories and I saw my calling as part of His plan for the world not just something to benefit me. And God didn't inspire John and me to welcome more children into our home until we were a united front and had completely given each other our hearts.

So often we get impatient when God doesn't answer our prayers like we want when we want. But I now understand that sometimes the gifts we long for would crush us if we aren't prepared for them. Jesus knows this and so He waits.

So if you are struggling with anything you've read in this chapter, pause and ask God to search your heart and show you if there's anything that shouldn't be there. Ask Him to cleanse you and make you whole so you can walk out His Word without reservation. Before you start with anything else in this book, start with your heart.

Maybe you're afraid of what will happen when you start exploring old feelings and relationships. Know you don't have to do it alone. First, if you have a few trusted friends, ask them to pray about it with you. When I opened up to those I trusted, I discovered many of them had faced similar struggles. I no longer felt alone. I knew my godly friends understood and would continue to ask Jesus to keep me strong.

Also, if you're afraid, know you can take that fear to God. First John 4:18 says, "There is no fear in love. But perfect love drives out fear, because fear has to do with punishment. The one who fears is not made perfect in love." God doesn't want to take you back to those dark places to discourage or punish you, but to express His love. When I looked back to the painful times and pictured Jesus there, I realized He had wanted me to turn to Him all along. And He wants us to turn to Him even now. Jesus knows that healing our pasts benefits our futures and helps us grow closer to Him and to those dearest to us.

BUT I DON'T HAVE KIDS OR A HUSBAND!

Maybe you're reading this chapter and don't think it relates to you. Wait, friend, it does! Whether you have a husband or children or not, you can embrace whomever God brings into your life and decide to beautifully impact the ones He asks you to love and serve.

In the Bible we discover God's idea of family expands far beyond father, mother, and child. Naomi cared for and guided her daughter-in-law Ruth after losing her husband and sons (book of Ruth). Godly women cared for the needs of Jesus and His disciples, as though they were part of their own families. These women even followed Jesus to Jerusalem and witnessed His death. Matthew 27:55 says, "Many women were there, watching from a distance. They had followed Jesus from Galilee to care for his needs."

Also, the apostle Paul never married or had children, yet he became the spiritual father to many. Paul embraced this role. "I am writing this not to shame you but to warn you as my dear children," he wrote in 1 Corinthians 4:14. Paul considered the believers in Corinth, and elsewhere, his children because he led them to faith in Christ.

In all of his letters Paul spoke with love and authority to those God brought into his life as family. In 1 Corinthians 14:15, he wrote, "Even if you had ten thousand guardians in Christ, you do not have many fathers, for in Christ Jesus I became your father through the gospel."

Paul was not the only apostle to consider himself a spiritual father. In 3 John 1:4 the apostle John wrote to his fellow believers: "I have no greater joy than to hear that my children are walking in the truth." Both men accepted those who God brought into their lives as family. They weren't connected by blood, or even through adoption decrees, but through the Spirit of Christ.

In my own life an important spiritual mentor was my Sunday school teacher Margo. She had no kids of her own, but she tended to those in her Sunday school class as if they were. She helped us memorize Scripture verses. She took us out to eat and cared about our lives. She invited us into her home.

Elisabeth Eliott also inspired me. Elisabeth's first husband, Jim, was killed in 1956 while attempting to make missionary contact with the violent Auca tribe, leaving Elisabeth and their infant daughter behind. Elisabeth continued to live among and minister to the nearby Quichua tribe after her husband's death. During that time she met two Auca women who lived with her and taught her the tribe's language. She then served as a missionary to the tribe that killed her husband. They became her family for two years. Her story shows us that family can be anyone God brings us in all types of circumstances. It's not our job to question, only to love and serve.

"I have one desire now—to live a life of reckless abandon for the Lord, putting all my energy and strength into it," said Elisabeth Elliot.[2] May each of us live and love with the same reckless abandon with whatever family God puts in our path here on earth.

No matter who God brings into our lives we consider to be family, we need to continually pray for God to bring our hearts home. At the end of our lives the items checked off our to-do list won't matter when compared to the people God brought into our lives. The impact we have to those closest to us will matter most.

Deadlines will come and go, but family is forever.

FOR REFLECTION

1. What is one thing you can do today to show your family they really matter?

2. Who has God brought into your life, beyond your family, you can love, support, and do life with?

3. How does the realization that God is a daily God, meeting us during each moment and providing for our needs, help you as you step out to follow Him and to walk out His Word?

ACTION STEPS

1. Is there anything in your heart holding you back from the rich life God calls you to? Whisper Psalm 139:23–25 as a prayer: "Search me, God, and know my heart; test me and know my anxious thoughts. See if there is any offensive way in me, and lead me in the way everlasting."

2. Write a note to your husband, your children, or a meaningful person in your life, sharing how much they mean to you. Also share your dreams of how God can use you together.

3. If you don't have a time of Bible reading and prayer with your family, set one up. If your children are old enough, plan together what you want to study to help you be more diligent in walking out God's directives.

4. Pray that God will take away any fears for the journey ahead and help you to walk faithful steps with Him by your side.

10

The Work You're Meant to Do

Remember when you were little and someone asked you, "What do you want to be when you grow up?" It's adorable when six-year-olds say things such as police officer, ballerina, astronaut, or president of the United States. But during high school, most of us settle on a more realistic career choice than POTUS. We evaluate our interests and strengths. We weigh the cost of college and studying, and settle on a career path. Like most of the decisions we make at that age, this choice usually centers on our own happiness.

As we mature, we realize life isn't just about us. Maybe, just maybe, God designed us for a purpose that will impact His kingdom. The purpose we all share as Christ-followers is to worship God, love Him, love others, and live a godly life. But God also gave us individual things to do with our unique gifts and talents.

"God does both the making and saving. He creates each of us by Christ Jesus to join him in the work he does, the good work he has gotten ready for us to do, work we had better be doing," we read in Ephesians 2:9–10 (THE MESSAGE). Just as our lives and stories can impact the world, so can our daily work. God places men and women in all types of jobs and industries so they can influence others for Christ. Too often we believe that only some people are called into Christian ministry and the rest of us are off the hook, but truthfully, no matter what we do for work, God called us there to make an impact for His kingdom.

My childhood dream of being a teacher changed when I was twenty years old and had my second baby. I'd attempted to attend college, but as a wife and mom of two, it was just too much. John was working and attending school, and we only had one car. Trying not to show how defeated I felt, I assured John I'd go back to college later. Secretly I worried that the rest of my life would revolve around cooking, cleaning, and childcare—not that there's anything wrong with that. It just wasn't what I'd pictured for my future.

When I landed on the idea of becoming a writer, that goal consumed me. I was driven to make something of myself. Thankfully, God showed me that anything I wrote wasn't about me after all. It just took me being available and teachable to figure that out.

AVAILABILITY AND TEACHABILITY

When I attended my first writers' conference in 1994, I felt as if I'd found my perfect career fit. I sat in awe of the professional authors and soaked in their encouraging messages and helpful advice. They made publication seem possible.

At that conference, I connected with fifteen other women, some published, most not yet. We created a prayer support network called One Heart. Every week these women emailed their prayer requests to me, then I compiled them into one email and sent them back out to our group. We shared life and writing struggles. When one of us felt like giving up, we encouraged her. And when one of us succeeded, we celebrated together!

Over and over again this group has demonstrated that when God calls us, He does not call us alone. Ecclesiasties 4:12 says, "A person standing alone can be attacked and defeated, but two can stand back-to-back and conquer. Three are even better, for a triple-braided cord is not easily broken" (NLT). What an honor to have fifteen women, with God at our group's core, supporting and encouraging me.

Whenever writing became too challenging, God reminded me of all the people in His Word whom He called to do specific jobs only to face trouble. Moses faced the ruler of an empire and then oversaw a nation of grumpy, disobedient people until the day he died. Esther was crowned queen only to put her life on the line to save her people. Jeremiah bore such empathy for God's chosen nation that he was called the weeping prophet. Daniel lived in exile and served a pagan king. And let's not forget the lion's den. Even amid challenges, each of these men and women sought God's face and was available to do His work. I longed to do that too.

I was beginning to realize that my work wasn't about what made me happy, what made me popular, or what made me rich (good thing!); it was about doing my best for God. Isaiah 6:8 says, "Then

I heard the voice of the Lord, saying, 'Whom shall I send? And who will go for us?' And I said, 'Here am I. Send me!'" That same call was mine ... and yours: to be available to do what God wants you to do.

"God did not direct His call to Isaiah—Isaiah overheard God saying, ... who will go for Us?'" wrote Oswald Chambers in the classic *My Utmost for His Highest*. "The call of God is not just for the special few, it is for everyone. Whether or not I hear God's call depends on the state of my ears; and what I hear depends upon my disposition."[1]

If God has a great plan and calling for your life, don't you want to know it? To fulfill it? While you need to seek God's desired fit, you also need to do whatever work God places before you with all you have. Willingly follow God's call, even when the path isn't clearly laid out. "In God's kingdom, calling trumps credentials every time! God does not call the qualified. He qualifies the called," says Mark Batterson. "And the litmus test isn't experience or expertise. It's availability and teachability. If you are willing to go when God gives you a green light, He will take you to inaccessible places to do impossible things."[2]

As the years passed, my writing goals shifted. I didn't simply want to learn to write well; I wanted my skills to advance God's kingdom. I didn't just want to know how to develop a strong plot for a novel; I longed to grip people's hearts and imaginations with messages of truth.

And while it would be wonderful to say that my path to publication became easier, it didn't. For a season I faced a long valley of rejection. There was also a moment when I felt God asking me to give it all up. My answer changed everything.

THE LONG VALLEY OF REJECTION

In the first five years of my writing career, I got close to getting a publishing contract many times, only to receive a final no. Then one winter's day, I attended a local writers' group. The guest speaker was Ellen Gunderson Traylor, an author of wonderful biblical fiction. Ellen shared about her writing and publication journey. She also spoke of surrender and relinquishment. She said, "After years of striving and rejection, I told God, 'This is yours, Lord. I'm tired of fighting for this. I desire You, Jesus, more than publication. If I never get a book published that's okay.'"

My gut tightened. I knew God was asking me to surrender to Him my desire to be published. I had to reach a place where I wrote simply because God had called me to write, not in order to see my name in print. Would I work with the same diligence if I was working for Jesus alone?

At home, I got on my knees and lifted my hands, palms up, to Him. "Take this, Jesus," I prayed. "If I never get published, that's okay. I want You more." I repeated this prayer until I meant it. Soon, Jesus's sweet peace came over me. Hope filled my heart, and I truly believed—deep, deep down—that God had a good plan for me, even if it had nothing to do with getting published.

How could it be that God wanted me to relinquish the very dreams He had placed inside my heart? Maybe because He knew that neither book contracts nor a wide readership would ever bring joy and contentment to my soul like He would. As Charles Spurgeon said, "Nothing teaches us about the preciousness of the Creator as much as when we learn the emptiness of everything else."[3]

Do you have a career goal that you just can't shake from your mind? Is there something you have always dreamed of doing, that hasn't yet become a reality? Maybe, like me, you wish everything would just fall into place. You don't understand why more doors slam shut than swing open.

Can I be candid? God doesn't need your success, just like He didn't need mine. What God wants is our hearts. He wants our surrender. He doesn't want us to work *for* Him; He wants to work *in* and *through* us. To Jesus, relationship is key. He knows the closer we draw toward Him the better we relate to everything, including the work He calls us to do. "Delight yourself in the LORD, and he will give you the desires of your heart," we read in Psalm 37:4 (ESV). And as we delight in Him, we discover *He* is the desire of our hearts.

When your own hard work alone generates the success, your satisfaction lasts only for a moment before you steam ahead toward the next goal. But if you make your role and calling about your unified work with Jesus, He'll bring true satisfaction to your soul.

As you dare to walk with Him, you'll discover your unique purpose one day at a time, one opportunity at a time. After I relinquished my desires to Jesus, I still wanted to be published, but instead of rushing ahead with every idea that popped into my mind (since that obviously hadn't worked), I started paying attention to the stories God brought along my path. And would you believe my first novel was about heartbreak, surrender, and discovering your true purpose after finding liberation for your soul?

FROM DUST AND ASHES

I can still smell the scent of spring that lingered in the air the day I strolled behind my guide, Willy Novy, and our translator down the narrow streets of St. Georgen, Austria. Flowers spilled out of window boxes, and an elderly woman in a scarf swept her front porch. Rows of pastel cottages lined the street. Neatly painted picket fences cast shadows on the roadway where I walked with slow, purposeful steps. The scene would have been idyllic except for the mission of the visit. I was researching the Gusen death camps that operated during World War II. The quaint cottages had housed Nazi officers and their families.

Willy was only a child when his family lived on a hillside that overlooked the camps. He shared the anguish he and his parents felt for the thin prisoners, draped in rags and working forced labor. As an eight-year-old boy, Willy smuggled food to as many captives as he could until the day he was caught. "A Nazi officer took me home with a gun to my head," Willy told me. "The SS officer told my family that if anyone was caught aiding the prisoners, our whole family would be killed."

Who am I to have the honor of being here, and to write about this? I thought. I felt unworthy to tell Willy's story.

When I returned home, the story of one Nazi officer's wife haunted my mind. She hated what had been happening in the camps, and after the German guards surrendered to the Americans, she was first to go through the gates to care for the prisoners. My retelling of her story became my first novel, *From Dust and Ashes*.

That World War II novel led to many others, and for each one I interviewed citizens, soldiers, and prisoners who'd lived through the events. This led me to Willy, who shared his stories as we toured the streets of St. Georgen. It led me to attend three World War II reunions, where I interviewed hundreds of veterans. It ultimately brought me face-to-face with Holocaust survivors, my tears joining theirs.

That God had used me to retell these stories overwhelmed me. One day I humbly asked Jesus, "Why me?" And I felt the answer deep in my Spirit: *Because, Tricia, you were once imprisoned in sin, and I was your great liberator. That's what these books are all about.*

From Dust and Ashes, *Night Song*, *Arms of Deliverance*, and *Dawn of a Thousand Nights* launched my career as a fiction writer, but they also changed me. After talking to Holocaust survivors, I became more thankful about everyday life. I was grateful I could cook meals for my children, read stories with them, and openly share my faith.

Interviewing veterans opened my eyes to how brave acts change everything. Because eighteen-year-old young men sailed across distant seas to fight evil causes, John and I raised our children in a free country and pursued our careers and ministries without hindrance. I cut my fiction-writing teeth on these stories. And they taught me that Philippians 4:19 holds true for small details, not just large needs: "And my God will meet all your needs according to the riches of his glory in Christ Jesus." In my writing career, God shows up—and sometimes He likes to show off.

THE MASTER OF EVERY DETAIL

God clearly showed off when I worked on my World War II novel *Dawn of a Thousand Nights*. One of the characters, Katrine, a Jew, is hiding, pretending to be Aryan. When she finds herself pregnant by an SS officer, officials take her to a Lebensborn home in Belgium. Young women went to these homes to have babies for the Third Reich. The Reich established ten of these places in Germany, nine in Norway, two in Austria, and one each in Belgium, Holland, France, Luxembourg, and Denmark.

For my novel, I focused on the Lebensborn home in Belgium. The only problem was that as I researched it, everything I found was in a language I couldn't read! I became discouraged and prayed: *Lord, You were in Belgium in 1942. Please help me to find the information I need or connect me with someone who can.*

The prayer had barely left my lips when a thought popped into my mind: *Don't I know someone from Belgium?* Roger was an expert on the Battle of the Bulge, and he'd been interviewing veterans too. I emailed him and told him about my story. Then I explained, "The only problem is that I can't find information about the Lebensborn home. Can you help?"

Less than twenty-four hours later a response from Roger arrived: "Yes, I am aware of the Lebensborn home. In fact, I grew up in the town that it's in. It is a museum now, and I know the director. What type of information do you need?"

Tears of joy filled my eyes. Out of all the people in the world, the man God connected me with was someone I already knew. A man who, unbeknownst to me, had grown up in the very town where my novel was set. What were the odds? There are no odds with God. God has shown me over and over that He is my partner on this writing journey.

A few years after I wrote *Arms of Deliverance*, I was working on the third novel of my Chronicles of the Spanish Civil War series, *A Whisper of Freedom*. I was stuck on research again. This time I was having trouble finding out about German pilots and planes from the Condor Legion.

Even before World War II, German fighters, under Hitler's command, assisted the Spanish dictator Francisco Franco. I needed details about a German Junker Ju.52/3. Again, I prayed. Again, I trusted that God would bring me the information I needed.

Around the same time, a stranger, Norm Goyer, emailed me. Norm was researching his family tree and wanted to know if we were related. I checked and, with regret, reported back that I could find no common relations. Somewhere in our conversation Norm mentioned his age and that he was a pilot. I did some mental calculations and asked if he had been a pilot in World War II.

Norm had just missed flying in that war. But after his pilot days he became the editor of a flight magazine, which allowed him to fly all types of airplanes. I dared to ask if he'd flown a Junker Ju.52/3. It was such a rare airplane that I was sure the answer would be no. I was wrong. Norm had flown one and knew all about them. He helped me craft the scene in my novel down to the smallest detail.

That time I didn't need to reach out to someone. God brought him to me! I realized then that God cares about even the smallest details of our lives and work.

Originally my writing goal was simply to get published, but when I surrendered my writing to God, He guided me to people whose stories He wanted me to tell, stories that should not be forgotten. I wouldn't trade anything for the hugs I've received from veterans, for their smiles as I looked into tear-filled eyes, or for their heartfelt words: "Thank you for taking time to listen to my story."

I'll never forget one of my first reader letters. A Swiss girl who'd read the German version of *From Dust and Ashes* wrote it. She wanted me to know that when my character Helene got on her knees to accept Christ, she did too.

I started with the goal of writing romance novels, but God's purpose for my writing was far greater than what I'd envisioned. God gives us the work, guides the work, and then shows us how much He cares about the work in wonderful and intimate ways. He enjoys helping us fulfill our dreams. He doesn't just send us off on our merry way; He delights in fulfilling His great purposes in and through us.

WHAT WORK ARE YOU MEANT TO DO?

What about you? What unique talents has God given to you? What work has He called you to do?

On his website, author and speaker Jeff Goins has a free download titled *Seven Signs You've Found Your Calling*. In it he says you know you've found your calling when:

1. It's familiar. A calling comes not just by *looking forward* to what you will do but also by *looking back* at what you've done.
2. It's something other people see in you. Sometimes, our vocations are most obvious to those who know us BEST.
3. It's challenging. It must be difficult enough that not everyone can do it.
4. It requires faith. It cannot be something so obvious that you can easily explain it. It must be mysterious.
5. It takes time. You have to fail your way in the right direction before you find it.
6. It's more than just one thing. And it integrates well with the rest of your life, not competing with but complementing your top priorities.
7. It's bigger than you. The task must be so large that without a team of people, you cannot complete it on your own.[4]

As you read through this list, what God-given dream rises to the surface? What dream does God desire to fulfill in and through you? Open a bakery? Write a novel? Start a nonprofit? Do missions work?

It's easy to verbalize a dream; it's harder to take the steps to walk it out. Why? We must leave the comfort zones we've created for ourselves. Fear comes when we picture our calling and our work *without* Jesus guiding us. We try to make it all about us, and about all we could accomplish on our own. When in truth, we have no idea what the journey ahead looks like.

Perhaps your dream will lead you down a path similar to what you envision. Then again, those first steps could be to just get you moving. Isaiah 55:8–9 says, "'My thoughts are nothing like your thoughts,' says the LORD. 'And my ways are far beyond anything you could imagine. For just as the heavens are higher than the earth, so my ways are higher than your ways and my thoughts higher than your thoughts'" (NLT).

When we say yes to our calling we accept and trust God's great vision for our lives, which is higher than our own. We see what needs to be accomplished and understand that none of it can be done without Jesus providing His wisdom and strength.

Why does Jesus want to be part of the process? Why didn't He just gift and enable us in one swoop? Because He knows we'd become independent and take the credit. We think our work is all about the finished result, but to Jesus, it's about *us*. We change as God uses us, empowers us, and guides us in our work. Our self-will takes a back seat to what God wants to do in the world. Faith replaces our doubt as we witness God show up time and time again.

I know this firsthand. I am content not because of what I've achieved but because I know God has a good plan for my life and my work—one He designed from the beginning of time. I would have settled for so much less. But I'm thankful God didn't let me.

Are you willing to relinquish your goals, dreams, calling, and talents to Him? If so you can't imagine where the journey will take you, one step at a time.

FOR REFLECTION

1. If you could do any type of work, what would it be?

2. Would you still be willing to work with the same diligence if it meant you would receive no benefit except for the knowledge you were working for Jesus alone?

3. Why do you think God asks us to relinquish the very dreams He's placed within our hearts?

4. Have you made yourself available to follow God's call in your work? If so, how has He already started to move in your heart and your experiences?

ACTION STEPS

1. Where do you feel God is guiding your calling and your work? What would your calling and your work look like if you walked alongside Him with every step? List some ways you can ensure you are walking alongside God rather than trying to take the lead.

2. What do you fear about following God's calling in your work? Write down your fears and turn them over to God.

3. Do you have a dream that has become an idol in your life? Relinquish that dream to God. Ask Him to take it. Trust that He'll either remove it because He has a better plan or He'll remake it to give Himself glory.

4. Research the ministry, vocation, or job you feel God is calling you to. Create a list of next steps you need to take to follow Him into that call.

11

On Earth as in Heaven

The first time I attended a multiethnic church was when John and I visited the International Church of Prague. As the service started, the pastor asked for any visitors to identify where they were from. Throughout the building answers rang out: "The United States." "Kenya." "China." "Ireland." And those are just the countries I remember.

As we worshipped together in song, our voices joining as one, goose bumps rose on my arms. *This is what heaven is going to be like.* I closed my eyes and listened to the various accents of the people around me. How amazing it was to travel around the world and worship with my brothers and sisters in Christ. As Romans 12:5 says, "So we, though many, are one body in Christ, and individually members one of another" (ESV).

As I gazed over this gathering of people with differing ethnicities and skin colors, I wished churches in the United States were similarly diverse. Dr. Martin Luther King Jr. is credited with saying that in the United States, Sunday at 11 a.m. is the most segregated hour of the week.[1] That's true in the South, where our family currently lives. We have white churches, black churches, and Hispanic churches. Many congregations believe they're diverse if a handful of families from another ethic background attend. While some churches work hard toward diversity, they are in the minority.

Should it be like this? I don't think so. It's important to God that men and women from all nations, tribes, and languages gather together in worship. How do we know this is important to Him? Because He gave us a glimpse of heaven. Revelation 7:9 says, "After this I looked, and there before me was a great multitude that no one could count, from every nation, tribe, people and language, standing before the throne and before the Lamb. They were wearing white robes and were holding palm branches in their hands."

Psalm 133:1 adds, "How good and pleasant it is when God's people live together in unity!"

If this is important to God, shouldn't it be important to us?

American Christians send out missionaries and support their travels around the world, yet how well do we connect with the person down the street who is of a different race or ethnicity from us? Not very. What are we doing to spread the gospel to people of different races and ethnicities inside our own country's borders? As I considered this question, I realized I needed to take it to heart.

I've always loved meeting people from different countries and learning about their lives and cultures, but for many years we lived in Montana where there was little ethnic diversity. The race problems we saw on TV seemed like a different world.

John and I were happy in our rural country church, where everyone was basically like us: middle class and white. Then we moved to Little Rock, where race issues weren't just a thing of the past, back during the civil rights movement. They are still a big issue today. And that's where a conflict arose within me. How could I believe that God desires His people to accept all people, yet attend a church with people who mostly looked just like me?

LIVE AT PEACE WITH EVERYONE

We'd only lived in Little Rock for a few weeks when I took my then sixteen-year-old son, Nathan, to the Central School Museum. This school was the site of forced school desegregation after the United States Supreme Court ruled in 1954 that public school segregation was unconstitutional. Nine black students, known as the Little Rock Nine, faced an angry mob of over a thousand white people who protested their entrance at the start of the new school year.

Police attempted to escort the children inside the school and violence erupted, so the black students were whisked away to safety. Instead of supporting the students, the Arkansas governor questioned the federal court system's authority to legislate desegregation. Most of the South pledged to resist the court's ruling. Yet someone even greater than the Arkansas governor had a say.

The day after the students were denied entrance, President Dwight D. Eisenhower ordered the United States Army's 101st Airborne Division to escort the nine students into the school. Melba Pattillo Beals, one of the nine students wrote in her diary, "After three full days inside

Central [High School], I know that *integration* is a much bigger word than I thought."[2]

Sixty years later I still felt the tension in Little Rock. Segregation was evident, especially on Sunday mornings. During the week John and I shopped with people of all ethnic and economic backgrounds, but when we went to church, we again found people just like us. Something didn't seem right about this.

I also noticed that the area we'd moved into (though we were unaware when we chose it) was mostly white too. It shocked us that we'd moved into such a diverse city, yet somehow found ourselves in a white, middle-class bubble.

This reminded me of my childhood, where the black families in our Northern California town lived in a neighborhood called Lincoln Heights. They even attended a black church. It seemed natural growing up. That's how things were back then, but as an adult it no longer seemed natural or right to me.

After all, God's feelings on the matter of segregation are clear: "There is neither Jew nor Gentile, neither slave nor free, nor is there male and female, for you are all one in Christ Jesus" (Gal. 3:28). We are one in Christ: black, white, Hispanic, and every other race and ethnicity. But I knew nothing would change in *my world* unless I made deliberate choices. I needed to make a conscious effort to walk out what this Scripture required.

It would have been easy for John and me to stay in our comfort zone: to buy a house in the neighborhood where people were just like us and to attend a church where people dressed, looked, talked, and acted the same. But I felt deep inside that I'd be ignoring God's heart for His people if I did that. If we were all one in Christ, my actions should show that. Our conscious changes started with where we attended church. And that one decision changed everything.

HEADING INTO THE INNER CITY

One day not long after our move, I lay in bed, praying about where we should attend church when a thought popped into my mind: *multi-ethnic church, Little Rock.* I sat up in bed. Was there such a thing? I ran to my computer, and I was both happy and surprised when I searched and something popped up. The first thing I read was an article from *Christianity Today* from 2005. This is how the article opened:

> Roaches occasionally crawl along the tile floor of the 80,000-square-foot space. The flags of 21 nations, representing the different nationalities of attendees, are all about the room. Sitting in the chairs are about 400 people, including a U.S. senator (Mark Pryor), a homeless man, a former NBA star, an undocumented alien, a local TV anchorwoman, a Middle Eastern convert from Islam, an attorney, a disabled teenager, a physician, an alcoholic, and a blind man. It is a mosaic of a church. In fact it is Mosaic Church of Central Arkansas.
>
> By his third year at a predominantly white megachurch in Little Rock, Mark DeYmaz had settled comfortably into his youth pastor position. But in 1997, the 40th anniversary of the integration of Little Rock schools, DeYmaz still felt some

attitudes had changed little in the Arkansas capital, which is 55 percent white and 40 percent black. He sensed God calling him to be a catalyst for change in this historic battleground for civil rights. By 2001, the church had held its first service.[3]

My heartbeat quickened as I read the article—and no it wasn't because of the cockroaches. The flags of twenty-one nations hanging in the building excited me, flags representing the countries of various members of the congregation. The opportunity to worship with an ethnically diverse congregation in a town that was historically a hotbed for racial segregation thrilled me.

GO WHERE THEY ARE

While I was enthusiastic about attending Mosaic Church, John wasn't so sure. Every week as we drove the twenty minutes to Mosaic, we passed dozens of other churches.

"Is it wrong to drive twenty minutes to a church when good ones exist within our own neighborhood?" he would ask.

"I don't think so," I told him. "There are no churches like *this one* near us." Still, he struggled with the question.

Then, one day he shared some new insights on the subject. "I've been praying about it, and I feel God has given me clarity," he began. "Jesus came to earth, to come where we are. He walked all over Israel—even to Samaria—during His time on earth, to be where people were." He smiled. "And that's why we drive into the inner city. Many of our members wouldn't travel out to a church in the suburbs. That's why we have to go where they are."

John put into words what I'd been feeling, but hadn't been able to verbalize. "Yes, just think of our teen mom support group," I added. "Even if the young moms had gas money and transportation, most of them wouldn't attend a meeting in the suburbs. They wouldn't feel comfortable. Yet they feel completely comfortable coming to the group at Mosaic, even though it is inside the church, because it's right next to the place they get gas and right across the street from the store where they grocery shop."

I remember John's words every time we drive into the inner city. *Yes, we must go where they are.* We not only attend church there, but our whole family (teens included) leads children's church every week. We go to Mosaic because we understand God's heart for all people from all ethnic and economic backgrounds. And when we go we experience things that encourage us, but also some things that challenge us.

SEEING THE WORLD IN A DIFFERENT WAY

After we started attending Mosaic and developing friendships with people from different ethnic backgrounds, I began seeing the world differently, through the lens of racism. For most of my life I thought racism was rare. I considered it a Southern problem or an inner-city problem, but I've come to realize that it's a bigger problem than most of us want to admit.

I clearly remember one church service in which Pastor DeYmaz discussed how white people often don't understand how blacks are treated in everyday life. He asked us to stand if a store employee had ever followed us through a store. He asked us to stand if a cop had ever pulled us over for no reason. He asked us to stand if our mamas had taught us to roll down the window and place our hands on the top of the steering wheel, or the top of our heads, where they could be seen when a police officer pulled us over. One by one, members of our congregation stood. All of them were black or Hispanic. Most were men.

My heartbeat quickened and the color drained from my face. I looked around noting Mike, Woodson, and Anthony, among others. These men were church elders and deacons. They have prayed over our family, and they greet each of us with hugs and smiles every week. Tears filled my eyes as I considered the way they'd been treated—not just in decades past—but in recent years.

It's not only my African American friends who face prejudice. My friend Alex is from Venezuela. As he's stood in the checkout line, he's had parents look at him suspiciously and pull their children closer to themselves, as if protecting them from him. Other times police tail him as he just drives through town. Alex is one of our pastors and one of the most God-fearing men I know. Could this really be happening in our country today? Of course, as a white female I don't see it, and I didn't know things like this still happened until I took time to pay attention, to listen, and to hear the stories.

Even worse is that the racism black and Hispanic youths deal with on a daily basis is ignored. We teach them Jesus is the answer and church is vital for their Christian walk, but can you imagine how they feel when the church stays silent as people of color continue to experience racial profiling and violence by authority figures?

Some youth walk away from both the church and its people, and seek answers in other places, like the streets, where they feel they have a better chance at being heard. Recently I read a blog written by a beautiful African American woman, and this is what she said:

> I haven't been to church in over a year now, and I've been pondering how I should address what I've discovered along the way. If you've been following my blog for a while, you probably could've never guessed that I would end up here. I never imagined that I could exist outside the Church I once held so dear. But due to the routine state-sanctioned violence that is being inflicted on my people, and the inadequate response from the church (among other things), I have decided to remove myself entirely from a system that claims to value my soul, but fails to show up for my Black body.[4]

The writer then lists twenty lessons she learned since leaving the church. They include: "Western Christianity is the farthest thing from what the original church sought out to accomplish," and "These pastors ain't loyal."[5] I understand where she's coming from. We claim to be the body of Christ, yet most of us don't acknowledge when one part of us is hurting.

This young woman is not alone in her feelings. Her words echo in my aching heart: "I've decided to remove myself entirely from a system that claims to value my soul, but fails to show up for my Black body." My initial response is to run and find an answer for her and others who feel that way. Just like I long to find an answer for the homeless church member who shows up without shoes or a coat on cold days or the teen mom who needs food. My desire to fix things—I've learned—is actually part of the problem. It's not about "us" (the middle-class majority) helping "them" (whatever minority that may be). It's all of us loving and serving each other.

Our church does a lot of outreach. We have food pantries, immigration services, and groups that help teen moms and those who age out of foster care. Middle-class whites can easily feel that we—and our programs—are the answer to a minority problem. But at our church it isn't the white people running the programs for everyone else. We all work together side-by-side, serving in the capacities God has given us.

During our Tuesday food bank, called The Orchard, a homeless volunteer works alongside the CEO of a company, also a volunteer. Men and women from all ethnic backgrounds serve together. And what do those visiting The Orchard witness? The church being the hands and feet of Jesus.

"What is the task of the church?" asks Steve Corbett, in his book *When Helping Hurts*. "We are to embody Jesus Christ by doing what He did and what He continues to do through us: declare—using both words and deeds—that Jesus is the King of kings and Lord of lords who is bringing in a kingdom of righteousness, justice, and peace. And the church needs to do this where Jesus did it, among the blind, the lame, the sick and outcast, and the poor."[6] And, I might add, among those who are racially different from us. Among those who our world attempts to divide. God's love for all people is not just a story we should *tell* in church, but rather something every member should *see* and *experience*: the love of Jesus unifying us and bringing us together.

One of the hardest things any of us face is going somewhere and feeling as if we don't fit in. Yet how wonderful it is to be welcomed, especially by those who look different from us. It's the Golden Rule walked out: "So in everything, do to others what you would have them do to you, for this sums up the Law and the Prophets" (Matt. 7:12).

Or as Jesus also put it, "'Love the Lord your God with all your heart and with all your soul and with all your strength and with all your mind'; and, 'Love your neighbor as yourself'" (Luke 10:27). This verse doesn't say, "Love your neighbor who looks just like you." It says, "Love your neighbor." And as someone who's received that type of love, I know what a difference it can make.

John and I have at times needed other people's kindness and generosity. While he was in college we struggled financially. More than once people brought food or slipped us a twenty-dollar bill. We felt loved, not pitied, and it made a big impact.

All people want to be treated with respect, even if they have great needs. They want to be cared for. They want to be listened to. This is true outside of the church, but it's even truer within its walls. People want to believe that the church cares for their physical bodies, just as much as it does their souls. They want us to show up and be present in their pain.

LOVE CHANGES THINGS

Love not only changes things. Love not only changes other people. Love also changes me. When I open up my mind and heart to other people from all backgrounds, I grow and change in the process. I learn to love better. I learn to care in different ways. I allow Jesus to love through me.

I love a teen girl named Leila who calls me Mom even though her skin is many shades darker than mine. I love my friend Jan who became my coleader in our teen MOPS ministry. Jan's great-grandfather was born into slavery, and when she was six years old she met him on his hundredth birthday. I love Shamim, who is from Kenya, grew up Muslim, and found Christ as a teen. Shamim offers me insight on being an immigrant and on cross-cultural issues. I love Benilda from Panama, who puts her painful, abusive childhood aside to roll up her sleeves and help anyone who needs it.

How do I love them? By listening to their stories and caring about their histories. By seeking to understand their challenges—and our differences—and making the effort to step forward with care and prayers. By lavishing them with hugs and cheering them on. And they love me back, doing the same for me.

Perfect love doesn't cast out differences. *Perfect love casts out fear.* Fear of misunderstandings. Fear of not getting our way. Fear of someone thinking differently than we are used to.

If we want people who are different from us to feel welcome in our church, then we need to show them love and friendship. "If Jesus is not enough for the church, why would he be enough for the world?" says author and speaker Christine Caine.[7]

As one of our church members, Phil Fletcher, recently said in a sermon, "Solidarity is love made public." My friends and I demonstrate love to a watching world when we support each other and cherish our friendships despite age, economic, ethnic, and cultural differences.

LISTEN AND ASK QUESTIONS

As I spend time with people of color, I've found the best thing I can do is ask questions and listen. I ask: How do you see the conflict that's happening on the news? What do you think of this new policy? What issues worry you that no one is talking about? What do you think people don't understand about racial divisions?

I've asked my African American friends to share their fears concerning police brutality, especially toward African American males, and here are a couple of examples of what they've said.

- "Will that be my son? I can teach him all I can about authority and respect, but I'm fearful that he'll be at the wrong place at the wrong time with the wrong person at the other end of the gun."
- "I don't understand how Christians can see what is happening, witness the injustice and the violence, and not do or say anything."

And after I listen, I also share my point of view as a daughter whose stepfather was a police officer during my growing up years. My background brought fears of my own. "It was scary seeing my dad put on his uniform every day and walk out the door," I've told a few friends. "I never knew what he'd face. I always hoped he'd come back."

Maybe thinking about having conversations like these makes you nervous, but with all that's happening in our country and in our world—and with all that's being reported in the news—even more tension builds when racial issues *aren't* spoken about. Our friends may wonder, "Doesn't she care about what's happening?"

At least raising the conversation shows we are listening and we do care, even if we don't have the answers.

And don't always focus on differences. We connect through similarities too. When we look for things we have in common we build a wonderful foundation for a relationship that can grow.

BUT I DON'T LIVE IN THE CITY!

Maybe, unlike me, you don't go to an inner-city church. Maybe you don't live in a part of the country that witnesses a lot of race issues. There are still ways you can build friendships and connect with others across ethnic and cultural lines.

Ask God to change your heart. Pray and ask that He helps you see the joy of unity and diversity in relationships. Ask Him to help you notice.

Get to know your neighbors. My neighbor Tracey is much better at this than I am. She owns a boxer and walks him in the morning and at night. As she walks, she stops and talks to people also out walking or who are working in their yards. She knows people all around our neighborhood, and she's been key in bringing people together.

Who lives in your community? Who is being included and who is being excluded? Whose voices are loud, and whose voices are silent? What are their challenges? What are their needs? Who might you take a step toward to build or grow a friendship? Can you invite someone into your home or join a new friend in an activity you both enjoy?

Reach out to your local college or university. Every year in the United States over one million international students come to study here.[8] They attend small community colleges and large universities, and often struggle to connect with people beyond their campuses. According to one study, 40 percent of students report they have no close American friends.[9] A statistic I've often heard quoted says that 80 to 90 percent of international students visiting the United States never enter an American home. The world is coming to our door, and we're ignoring it.

Connect with a coworker. Do you have a coworker whose race or cultural background differs from yours? Go out of your way to open up conversations and build a friendship.

Host an exchange student. Our family hosted an exchange student from the Czech Republic the year after our first mission trip there. She lived in our home for nine months, during the school year. Andrea is forever considered one of our kids, and our family learned so much about her life and culture during her stay with us.

Build family relationships with the families of kids on your child's sports team or in their school. Make an effort to reach out to families whose children have similar ages and hobbies as yours. Most children naturally look beyond race and cultures when making friends, and we should follow their example.

Try to understand another's history. See your new friend as an individual and not a stereotype. And even if you mess up and commit a cultural faux pas, the relationship you've created will make it easier for both of you to laugh off your mistakes.

One of my favorite books of recent years was *The Warmth of Other Suns* by Isabel Wilkerson. This book chronicles the decades-long migration of black citizens who fled the South for northern and western cities, in search of a better life. The stories shared were lovely, heartbreaking, and shocking.

Reading books like this has helped me understand the injustice and fear in my community and my country. The racial and socioeconomic issues in the news today didn't happen overnight. Instead, they are old issues that society has pushed under the surface for too long. Laws or government programs won't fix them. They will only be solved by individual people changing and asking God to show them His heart. When our awareness of God's heart for diversity and unity expands, we realize reconciliation is not someone else's problem, but ours.

These are a few ideas for building connections and friendship across ethnic and cultural lines, but don't stop there—keep learning, educating yourself, and asking God how He wants you to walk out this mandate.

SO MUCH TO LEARN

Personally, I feel as if I am just scratching the surface in embracing racial diversity. I need to listen, connect, and embrace more. But I'm willing to keep working at it. Why? Because I'm choosing God's great purpose—unity.

My friend Jan recently said to me, "I find that churches are worshipping on Sunday together and call it unity, but we still don't go home with each other through the week. So that seems hypocritical. I believe unity starts in your home. Can we do life together?" "Doing life together" suggests being in each other's homes and connecting with each other outside of church.

Our goal for the coming months and years should reach beyond enjoying worshipping with each other at church (although that is a wonderful start), to also doing life together more often. This means all of us must spend more time with people who are different from us, welcoming each other into our homes and having conversations that matter about all types of topics.

Most likely we won't do this perfectly. We'll probably say insensitive things or put our foot in our mouths more than once, because that's how relationships work. But it'll be worth it. The closer we grow to people who differ from us, the more we're able to understand racial and other struggles in our world.

Lately I've been cultivating a friendship with Tracey, who has lived in my neighborhood for years. I join her in her morning walk several days a week. Tracey and I come from different walks of life and different backgrounds, but we enjoy our time together. We talk about everything from our growing-up experiences, our favorite recipes, and the cultural struggles in our city. We talk every day and are in each other's homes multiple times a week. I watch her son when she needs help, and she takes my kids out for fun outings, like dinner dates and campouts. I wish I'd made the effort to know her sooner.

I didn't reach out to her sooner because she's a highly educated, single mom who works full-time. She's also black and I'm white, and for some reason I expected to find more differences than similarities. I'd assumed we'd hold different opinions about racial issues and politics. I doubted we'd have much to talk about, but I was wrong. We both enjoy cooking and caring for our kids. We like to travel and read. Yes, we've had conversations about race, but they've always been respectful and caring.

As I'm choosing to walk out God's desire that we live in unity with *all* people, I'm modeling for my children a better way to live. I'm helping them understand their heavenly Father's heart.

UNDERSTANDING THE FATHER'S HEART

God desires us to live together in unity with all people. As a mom, I've always understood this desire for unity, and recognize it extends to my immediate family as well. I want my kids to love each other and get along because I know that someday I'll be gone and all they'll have is each other, until we're united again in paradise.

But when I became an adoptive mom, I understood this even more. We've brought children together from various backgrounds, and we want them to see themselves as part of our family.

At times our children have attempted to label themselves and each other, saying things like, "I'm only getting Christmas gifts for my *biological* sisters." We stop such talk. According to the courts and legal documents, all of our children are Goyers, no matter if they came to be part of our family via the birth canal or the courts.

Similarly, God loves every person on this earth equally. He made us all in His image, no matter if we look alike or don't. We're all His regardless of where we came from or how we view our present or our future. We are all the same in God's eyes. His children: chosen, loved, petitioned for, and paid for with the blood of Jesus.

Many Christ-followers want to do something about the racial divides. What can we do? We can walk it out. Unity within the body of Christ—and within our communities—isn't something to tack on; it must become who we are. And what happens when we make this a priority? We become light to a dark world. A world that since the beginning of recorded history has been divided by race and social status.

What can we do? We can ask Jesus to show us His heart for unity. We can be a bridge by reaching out to a person of a different race or ethnicity than us. We can each exemplify Christ-at-work, bringing all things together in a diverse world. And we can make St. Francis of Assisi's prayer our own:

Lord, make me an instrument of your peace.
Where there is hatred, let me bring love.
Where there is offense, let me bring pardon.
Where there is discord, let me bring union.
Where there is error, let me bring truth;
Where there is doubt, let me bring faith.
Where there is despair, let me bring hope;
Where there is darkness, let me bring your light;
Where there is sadness, let me bring joy.

O Master,
let me not seek as much
To be consoled, as to console;
To be understood, as to understand;
To be loved as to love.

For it is in giving that one receives,
It is in self-forgetting that one finds,
It is in pardoning that one is pardoned;
It is in dying that one is raised to eternal life. Amen.[10]

FOR REFLECTION

1. Why do you think unity in His body—the church—is important to God?

2. In what ways does our unity as believers reflect Christ's love to a waiting world?

3. What would becoming an instrument of peace look like in your neighborhood or community?

ACTION STEPS

1. Find someone to connect with, either a coworker, international student, or neighbor. Begin building a friendship based on your similarities, and then move toward understanding each other's differences.

2. Educate yourself on the race issues happening in your community, around the country, and around our world. Start conversations with those who you know are impacted. Let them know that even though you may not completely understand, you care.

3. Volunteer at a local community organization. Get to know the other volunteers and those you serve, not only to provide the answers but to understand.

4. Read a book such as *The Warmth of Other Suns* by Isabel Wilkerson to discover a part of history you may not know.

CONCLUSION

A Daily God

How do you feel now that you've reached the end of this book? Excited and eager to discover where walking out God's Word will take you? Scared about what God is going to ask you to do? Maybe a mix of both? I understand. Even though this book is ending, my walk with God isn't. Even as I write these words God has new paths planned for me—ones I'm both happy and nervous to discover. But I've come far enough to know that whatever lies ahead is not about me.

We sometimes think our job on earth is to figure out what God wants from us and to do it. Instead, I've discovered that walking out all God asks of us involves being connected on a daily basis with our God, who interacts with us in that day-to-day. It's also seeing that all parts of our lives benefit the other parts. For instance, I am the writer I am because I'm the mom I am. And I am the mom I am because I'm the writer I am. In the strange way God works, one role needs the other.

Jesus loves me so much that He gave me kids I'd fall in love with, even in the midst of very hard stuff. He gave me books and articles to write, not just to benefit others but also to benefit me. He's led me to a place where I can't take another step without Him, because everything is just too big to handle alone. And this is exactly where He wants me to be.

Many believers fear stepping out to follow God, scared of getting hurt, losing safety, looking bad, failing—or even succeeding. They don't want to take on more than they think they can handle, and they've forgotten God is with them. They believe they have to do everything in their own strength and under their own power. Yet God wants to be with us on a daily basis.

Dare I say it? Sometimes we step out of God's will for us today because we're trying to figure out what He has planned for us tomorrow—for our future. But when we walk out God's directives and take steps of self-sacrifice, love, service, and compassion, we *will* discover God's purpose for our future, and our family's future, because our faithful steps will lead us to it.

"Who we choose to become and how we choose to live every day creates a trajectory for everything else," said author Jerry Sittser. "Perhaps that is why the Bible says so little about God's will for tomorrow and so much about what we should do to fulfill his will today."[1]

Only when I sat down to write about all God has done in my life did I realize that each area of blessing leads back to a moment of relinquishment and obedience. And each act of obedience stemmed from one of God's directives in Scripture.

All of us have moments when we come upon a special verse and our hearts twinge. It's up to us to either keep reading or to pause and wonder what message Jesus has for us within those words. I'm so glad that in each of the areas I mentioned I paused to dig deeper with God, allowing Him not only into my heart but into my life—and my family's life—as I've walked those words out.

I encourage you, friend, to turn to God's Word every day with a heart to listen and a mind to obey. Yes, God may sometimes call you to something beyond your natural bent or abilities, but trust that as you follow Him you'll discover more about yourself and your capabilities than you ever dreamed possible. More than that, you'll discover more about God—His character and His ways.

And that's the adventure of a lifetime: to know Christ and to be known and cared for by Him. Through these paths God has taken me on He's revealed His heart in ways I never could have experienced on my own. He's protected my family and me; He's shielded us and guarded our paths as we've stepped forward in faithfulness. The closer I walk to Him, the less frequently I wander off. The less often my feet take me to trouble, drama, and destruction.

As I follow His paths today, God reveals Himself in little moments. I come across the perfect Scripture verse. I hear a meaningful worship song. I receive an encouraging note from a friend, which says just what I needed to hear—and confirms God's message to me—and I find myself stepping forward more and more in faith and without fear.

I've seen God show up time and time again to rescue and provide in my work and in the ministries I serve, and I know He'll continue to do so as I step forward in obedience.

Proverbs 2:1–9 confirms what I've lived out:

My child, listen to what I say, and treasure my commands. Tune your ears to wisdom, and concentrate on understanding. Cry out for insight, and ask for understanding. Search for them as you would for silver; seek them like hidden treasures. Then you will understand what it means to fear the LORD, and you will gain knowledge of God. For the LORD grants wisdom! From his mouth come knowledge and understanding. He grants a treasure of common sense to the honest. He is a shield to those who walk with integrity. He guards the paths of the just and protects those who are faithful to him. Then you will understand what is right, just, and fair, and you will find the right way to go. (NLT)

My desire for you is that as you read God's Word and do what it says, God will lead you in faithful steps. Also remember, you don't have to journey alone. This is a journey God is asking you to walk with Him. It's a journey of purpose. It's a journey of faith. It's a journey that will change everything about your life, and your family's life, in ways you'll never imagine. Here is my prayer for you and for me:

> *Dear Jesus,*
>
> *Pour out Your presence to us today, and speak through Your Word. May You become known to us as we seek You. Guide us in understanding what makes Your heart break. Help us to reach out to others as we obey. Help us to love and serve as You would here on earth.*

Forgive us, Lord, for all the times we've put our own comfort and desires before following You. Thank You, Lord, for Your gentleness in leading us. You don't force us or twist our arms. Instead You stir our hearts and direct us with Your love.

We know the lives of others will be transformed as we step forward in obedience, but more importantly we understand our minds, hearts, spirits, and life's purposes will be changed.

It's impossible to touch the eternal love of Christ and exhibit His grace without becoming more like You. Yet with You, Jesus, in us and through us, we can do all things in Your strength. May those "all things" be given to You as an offering. And may we glimpse Your pleasure as we take our feeble steps, so we may not be discouraged along the way.

Help us to dare to read Your Word and follow it. And through our bravery may Your eternal kingdom be impacted for good.

In Jesus's name. Amen.

Walk it out, friend. Walk it out beautifully, with Jesus by your side.

Notes

INTRODUCTION

1. "Catherine Marshall Quotes," *Goodreads*, accessed April 11, 2017, www.goodreads.com/author/quotes/11237.Catherine_Marshall.

CHAPTER 1

1. I share my story in my book *Teen Mom: You're Stronger Than You Think* (Grand Rapids, MI: Zondervan, 2015).

2. "27 Hudson Taylor Quotes," ChristianQuotes.info, accessed December 17, 2016, www.christianquotes.info/quotes-by-author/hudson-taylor-quotes /#axzz4kUCG5JNW.

CHAPTER 2

1. Christa Black Gifford, *Heart Made Whole: Turning Your Unhealed Pain into Your Greatest Strength* (Grand Rapids, MI: Zondervan, 2016), 33.

2. Linda Cochrane, *Forgiven and Set Free: A Post-Abortion Bible Study for Women* (Grand Rapids, MI: Baker, 2015).

3. Dan B. Allender and Tremper Longman, *The Cry of the Soul: How Our Emotions Reveal Our Deepest Questions about God* (Colorado Springs: NavPress, 2015), 38.

CHAPTER 3

1. Amy Carmichael, *Candles in the Dark: Letters of Amy Carmichael* (Fort Washington, PA: Christian Literature Crusade, 1982), 53.

CHAPTER 4

1. Jerry L. Sittser, *A Grace Disguised: How the Soul Grows through Loss* (Grand Rapids, MI: Zondervan, 2004), 79.
2. *The Scottish Christian Herald* (Edinburgh: John Stonestreet, 1841), 377.

CHAPTER 5

1. Ann Voskamp, *The Broken Way: A Daring Path into the Abundant Life* (Grand Rapids, MI: Zondervan, 2016), 87.
2. Robert Madu, "The Best Quotes from Day 1 of Catalyst," *Ministry Grid* (blog), October 3, 2014, www.ministrygrid.com/blog/-/blogs/the-best-quotes -from-day-1-of-catalyst.
3. Matt Chandler, The Best Quotes from Day 1 of Catalyst," *Ministry Grid* (blog), October 3, 2014, www.ministrygrid.com/blog/-/blogs/the-best-quotes -from-day-1-of-catalyst.

CHAPTER 6

1. Henry Blackaby and Richard Blackaby, *Experiencing God* (Nashville: Broadman & Holman, 1990), 185.
2. Henry T. Blackaby, Claude V. King, and Richard Blackaby, *Experiencing God: Knowing and Doing the Will of God, Revised and Expanded* (Nashville: LifeWay, 2007), 123.

CHAPTER 7

1. Steve Corbett and Brian Fikkert, *When Helping Hurts: How to Alleviate Poverty without Hurting the Poor … and Yourself* (Chicago: Moody, 2009), 62.
2. Emily Badger, "How Poverty Taxes the Brain," *The Atlantic CityLab*, August 29, 2013, www.citylab.com/work/2013/08/how-poverty-taxes-brain/6716/.

CHAPTER 8

1. Amy L. Sherman, *Sharing God's Heart for the Poor: Meditations for Worship, Prayer and Service* (Charlottesville, VA: Trinity Presbyterian Church—Urban Ministries, 2000), Kindle edition, chap. 8.

2. Sherman, *Sharing God's Heart for the Poor*.

3. Watchman Nee, *Serve in Spirit*, (New York: Christian Fellowship Publishers, Inc., 2015), 12.

4. Philip Yancey, *Prayer: Does It Make Any Difference?* (Grand Rapids, MI: Zondervan, 2006), 105.

CHAPTER 9

1. Michael Burlingame, *The Inner World of Abraham Lincoln* (Urbana, IL: University of Illinois, 1997), 137.

2. Elisabeth Elliot, *Through Gates of Splendor* (Bromley, Kent: STL, 1988), 51.

CHAPTER 10

1. Oswald Chambers, *My Utmost for His Highest* (Westwood, NJ: Barbour and Company, 1963), January 14.

2. Mark Batterson, *All In: You Are One Decision Away from a Totally Different Life* (Grand Rapids, MI: Zondervan, 2013), 107.

3. Charles H. Spurgeon and Alistair Begg, *Evening by Evening: A New Edition of the Classic Devotional Based on the Holy Bible, English Standard Version* (Wheaton, IL: Crossway, 2007), November 19.

4. Jeff Goins, "Seven Signs You've Found Your Calling [Exclusive Content]," *Goins, Writer* (blog), October 23, 2014, www.goinswriter.com/calling-bonus-ty.

CHAPTER 11

1. Bob Smietana, "Sunday Morning Segregation: Most Worshipers Feel Their Church Has Enough Diversity," *Christianity Today*, January 15, 2015, www.christianitytoday.com/gleanings/2015/january/sunday-morning -segregation-most-worshipers-church-diversity.html.

2. Melba Pattillo Beals, *Warriors Don't Cry* (New York: Simon & Schuster, 2007), 113.

3. John W. Kennedy, "Big Dream in Little Rock," *Christianity Today*, April 1, 2005, www.christianitytoday.com/ct/2005/april/24.42.html.

4. Makiah Green, "20 Lessons I've Learned Since Leaving The Church," *The Huffington Post*, July 26, 2016, www.huffingtonpost.com/makiah-green/20-lessons-ive-learned-si_b_11199786.html.

5. Green, "20 Lessons I've Learned Since Leaving The Church."

6. Steve Corbett and Brian Fikkert, *When Helping Hurts: How to Alleviate Poverty without Hurting the Poor ... and Yourself* (Chicago, IL: Moody, 2009), 14.

7. Christine Caine, "The Best Quotes from Day 1 of Catalyst." Ministry Grid (blog), October 3, 2014, www.ministrygrid.com/blog/-/blogs/the-best-quotes-from-day-1-of-catalyst.

8. Kathleen Struck, "U.S. Hosts More than 1 Million International Students." *Student Union* (blog), November 15, 2016, blogs.voanews.com/student-union/2016/11/15/u-s-hosts-more-than-1-million-international-students/.

9. Scott Jaschik, "Friendless in America," *Inside Higher Ed*, June 14, 2012, www.insidehighered.com/news/2012/06/14/new-study-finds-many-foreign-students-lack-american-friends.

10. "Prayer of St. Francis," Wikipedia, last modified April, 15, 2017, https://en.wikipedia.org/wiki/Prayer_of_Saint_Francis.

CONCLUSION

1. Jerry L. Sittser, *The Will of God as a Way of Life: Finding and Following the Will of God* (Grand Rapids, MI: Zondervan, 2000), 25.